Joseph Barber Lightfoot

Leaders in the Northern Church, sermons preached in the Diocese of Durham

Joseph Barber Lightfoot

Leaders in the Northern Church, sermons preached in the Diocese of Durham

ISBN/EAN: 9783744746656

Printed in Europe, USA, Canada, Australia, Japan

Cover: Foto ©Lupo / pixelio.de

More available books at **www.hansebooks.com**

LEADERS IN THE NORTHERN CHURCH

LEADERS IN THE NORTHERN CHURCH

SERMONS PREACHED IN

THE DIOCESE OF DURHAM

BY THE LATE

JOSEPH BARBER LIGHTFOOT, D.D., D.C.L., LL.D.,
LORD BISHOP OF DURHAM

PUBLISHED BY THE TRUSTEES OF THE LIGHTFOOT FUND

London
MACMILLAN AND CO.
AND NEW YORK
1891

First Edition 1890
Reprinted 1891

Extract from the last Will and Testament of the late Joseph Barber Lightfoot, Lord Bishop of Durham.

"I bequeath all my personal Estate not herein-
"before otherwise disposed of unto [my Executors]
"upon trust to pay and transfer the same unto the
"Trustees appointed by me under and by virtue of a
"certain Indenture of Settlement creating a Trust to
"be known by the name of 'The Lightfoot Fund for
"the Diocese of Durham' and bearing even date
"herewith but executed by me immediately before
"this my Will to be administered and dealt with by
"them upon the trusts for the purposes and in the
"manner prescribed by such Indenture of Settle-
"ment."

Extract from the Indenture of Settlement of 'The Lightfoot Fund for the Diocese of Durham.'

"Whereas the Bishop is the Author of and is
"absolutely entitled to the Copyright in the several
"Works mentioned in the Schedule hereto, and for the

"purposes of these presents he has assigned or intends forthwith to assign the Copyright in all the said Works to the Trustees. Now the Bishop doth hereby declare and it is hereby agreed as follows:—

"The Trustees (which term shall hereinafter be taken to include the Trustees for the time being of these presents) shall stand possessed of the said Works and of the Copyright therein respectively upon the trusts following (that is to say) upon trust to receive all moneys to arise from sales or otherwise from the said Works, and at their discretion from time to time to bring out new editions of the same Works or any of them, or to sell the copyright in the same or any of them, or otherwise to deal with the same respectively, it being the intention of these presents that the Trustees shall have and may exercise all such rights and powers in respect of the said Works and the copyright therein respectively, as they could or might have or exercise in relation thereto if they were the absolute beneficial owners thereof....

"The Trustees shall from time to time, at such discretion as aforesaid, pay and apply the income of the Trust funds for or towards the erecting, rebuilding, repairing, purchasing, endowing, supporting, or providing for any Churches, Chapels, Schools, Parsonages, and Stipends for Clergy, and

"other Spiritual Agents in connection with the
"Church of England and within the Diocese of
"Durham, and also for or towards such other pur-
"poses in connection with the said Church of
"England, and within the said Diocese, as the
"Trustees may in their absolute discretion think fit,
"provided always that any payment for erecting any
"building, or in relation to any other works in con-
"nection with real estate, shall be exercised with due
"regard to the Law of Mortmain; it being declared
"that nothing herein shall be construed as intended
"to authorise any act contrary to any Statute or
"other Law....

"In case the Bishop shall at any time assign to
"the Trustees any Works hereafter to be written or
"published by him, or any Copyrights, or any other
"property, such transfer shall be held to be made for
"the purposes of this Trust, and all the provisions
"of this Deed shall apply to such property, subject
"nevertheless to any direction concerning the same
"which the Bishop may make in writing at the time
"of such transfer, and in case the Bishop shall at any
"time pay any money, or transfer any security, stock,
"or other like property to the Trustees, the same
"shall in like manner be held for the purposes of this
"Trust, subject to any such contemporaneous direc-
"tion as aforesaid, and any security, stock or pro-

"perty so transferred, being of a nature which can
"lawfully be held by the Trustees for the purposes
"of these presents, may be retained by the Trustees,
"although the same may not be one of the securities
"hereinafter authorised.

"The Bishop of Durham and the Archdeacons of
"Durham and Auckland for the time being shall be
"*ex-officio* Trustees, and accordingly the Bishop and
"Archdeacons, parties hereto, and the succeeding
"Bishops and Archdeacons, shall cease to be Trus-
"tees on ceasing to hold their respective offices, and
"the number of the other Trustees may be increased,
"and the power of appointing Trustees in the place
"of Trustees other than Official Trustees, and of
"appointing extra Trustees, shall be exercised by
"Deed by the Trustees for the time being, provided
"always that the number shall not at any time be
"less than five.

"The Trust premises shall be known by the name
"of 'The Lightfoot Fund for the Diocese of Durham.'"

PREFACE TO THE FIRST EDITION.

FOR many years past it had been Bishop Lightfoot's intention to publish some time or other a volume of sermons bearing upon the history of the Diocese of Durham.

A memorandum in his handwriting gives the whole series sketched out as follows: (1) The Celtic Mission of Iona and Lindisfarne, (2) S. Columba, (3) S. Oswald, (4) S. Aidan, (5) S. Hilda, (6) S. Cuthbert, (7) The Life of Bede, (8) The Death of Bede, (9) Benedict Biscop, (10) Antony Bek, (11) Richard de Bury, (12) Bernard Gilpin, (13) John Cosin, (14) Joseph Butler. Of these proposed sermons, the second, seventh, ninth and tenth were never written. In the present volume, which has been edited for the Trustees of the Lightfoot Fund by the Rev. J. R. Harmer, M.A., Fellow of Corpus Christi College, Cambridge, and Chaplain to the late Bishop, the series is now given to the world in its incomplete form, and a few notes have been added in illustration of some of the historical allusions.

September 13, 1890.

PREFACE TO THE SECOND EDITION.

A SERMON on S. Columba recently preached by the present Bishop of Durham has been added as an Appendix to this edition. Thus one of the gaps left by Bishop Lightfoot in the series as originally contemplated by him is now opportunely filled.

January 23, 1891.

CONTENTS.

                                                                             PAGE

I. THE CELTIC MISSION OF IONA AND LINDISFARNE.

Look unto the rock whence ye are hewn.

                                    ISAIAH li. 1. . 1

II. S. OSWALD.

Like unto him was there no king before him, that turned to the Lord with all his heart, and with all his soul, and with all his might.

                                   2 KINGS xxiii. 25.

Kings shall be thy nursing fathers.

                                  ISAIAH xlix. 23. . 19

III. S. AIDAN.

The glory of children are their fathers.

                                  PROVERBS xvii. 6. . 37

IV. S. HILDA.

I arose, a mother in Israel.

                                   JUDGES v. 7. . 55

V. S. CUTHBERT.

A thousand years in Thy sight are but as yesterday.

                                   PSALM xc. 4. . 71

CONTENTS.

VI. THE DEATH OF BEDE.
It is finished.
S. JOHN xix. 30. . 87

VII. RICHARD DE BURY.
Let us now praise famous men and our fathers that begat us....Their seed shall remain for ever, and their glory shall not be blotted out. Their bodies are buried in peace; but their name liveth for evermore.
ECCLESIASTICUS xliv. 1, 13, 14. . 103

VIII. BERNARD GILPIN.
Be ye thankful.
COLOSSIANS iii. 15. . 121

IX. JOHN COSIN.
Thou shalt be called the repairer of the breach, the restorer of paths to dwell in.
ISAIAH lviii. 12. . 137

X. JOSEPH BUTLER.
And they shall see His face.
REVELATION xxii. 4. . 159

APPENDIX. S. COLUMBA.
They that seek the Lord shall not want any good thing.
PSALM xxxiv. 10.
(Sermon by the Right Reverend B. F. WESTCOTT, D.D., D.C.L., Lord Bishop of Durham) . . 173

NOTES 191

THE CELTIC MISSION

OF

IONA AND LINDISFARNE.

D. S.

PREACHED IN THE CATHEDRAL CHURCH OF S. NICHOLAS, NEWCASTLE-UPON-TYNE, IN THE OCTAVE OF THE DEDICATION SERVICES.

November 20, 1887.
　Twenty-fourth Sunday after Trinity.

Look unto the rock whence ye are hewn.
ISAIAH li. 1.

AT a great crisis in their national history the prophet directs the thoughts of the chosen people to the lessons of a remote past. He bids them find inspiration and guidance in the first beginnings of their race. They were separated by a chasm of twelve or thirteen centuries from the day when their shepherd forefather left his far-off Syrian home to grasp the splendid destiny which God's purpose had marked out for his race. Yet this long interval, with its amazing vicissitudes, had not broken the continuity of their national life. The prosperity of a Church, as of a Nation, depends largely on its connexion with the past. Progress is not severance. A healthy Church is not indeed the slave, but it is essentially the child and the pupil, of the past. The accumulated lessons of its bygone history are its rich inheritance, lessons learnt alike from its failures and its successes.

Shall I do wrong then, if, on this last morning of

your dedication festival, I plant my foot in the prophet's tracks, and invite you, the latest sons and daughters of the Northumbrian Church, to look to the rock whence you were hewn, to glance for a few moments at the earliest history—the Celtic period—of the Northumbrian Church, and to draw thence the inspiring lessons which it promises to yield? In this octave of dedication services you celebrate the transformation of the ancient parish church into the cathedral of a new diocese; but this building, so transformed, is the outward embodiment, the local symbol, of the latest development of the Northumbrian Church—the foundation of the see of Newcastle. Is it not then an opportune moment to revert to the cradle of its history, and thus link together the last days with the first in the bonds of a natural piety? In this long lapse of time much has happened. The English Crown, the English Parliament, the English Nation itself, have come into being. But what then? The interval between this latest growth of the Northumbrian Church and its earliest beginnings is roughly the same as that which separated the prophet's utterance in the text from the call of Abraham, the forefather of the race. The value of the lessons is only increased by the lapse of time.

And indeed there has been no more brilliant epoch in the history of Northumbria than those earliest days. Northumbria has never since been so great a power in England, or indeed in Christendom, as she was in that remote age. Northumbria bore the chief part in the making of the English Church, as she did likewise in the making of the English State.

Shall I be thought to overstrain my analogy, if I begin by comparing the migration of S. Columba[1] from his Irish home to the migration of Abraham from Ur of the Chaldees, the one the initiative of the Northumbrian Church, as the other was the initiative of the Israelite people? A voluntary exile, like the patriarch of old, he obeyed the Divine call, and went forth, not knowing whither he went. He chose, we are told, as his adopted home the lonely, sterile, unlovely island which henceforth was to bear his name, because from its shores he could no longer gaze on the country which he loved with a tender, passionate love. Passionate indeed he was; passionate in his wrath, as he was passionate in his love. His was no faultless character. He had all the defects and all the virtues of his race in a heightened form. He was headstrong alike in his attractions and his repulsions—now fierce in his vindictiveness and now melting into tenderness—a nature of the strongest contrasts, a fountain sending forth both sweet water and bitter. But it is not for us members of the Northumbrian Church to lay our finger on the dark blots which stained so beautiful a picture. If he was not an apostle, not a saint, to others, at least to us, the heirs of his self-devotion, he was both in the highest degree. It is far pleasanter to note how the beauty of his character shone out, and the ugliness vanished, under the influence of his evangelistic work in his self-chosen exile. The very incident which led to this exile reveals the strong contrasts in his nature. He had a quarrel about the possession of a Psalter, which he considered to have been wrongly adjudged to another. He stirred up a deadly strife between clan and clan to avenge the wrong. Overwhelmed with penitence, he pledged himself to win as many souls to Christ, as bodies had been slain in the murderous conflict. His exile was the expiation of this sin, the redemption of this pledge. 'It is thou who art my father,' said the faithful disciple[2] who accompanied him: 'I swear to follow thee, wherever thou goest.' 'My country is where I can gather the largest harvest for Christ.' The words of the disciple reflect the spirit of the teacher.

And so the harvesting of souls for Christ began. For thirty long years Iona was the centre of his evangelistic work. Never man laboured more earnestly or more successfully for Christ. When the sixth century was fast drawing to its close he passed away, some three or four weeks after Augustine had landed on the shores of Kent. His missionary work was altogether independent of Rome. The Roman legions had long been withdrawn from Britain. They had never penetrated into Ireland. But the influence of the Roman Church was largely dependent on the extension of the Roman Empire. Hence Celtic Christianity grew up, a strictly native growth. The influence of Rome for long centuries was practically unfelt. Whether for good or for evil, the Island of the Saints developed a type of Christian civilisation and Christian character peculiar to itself. Long after the English Church had submitted to the Roman domination, the Irish Church remained essentially free. It was not till the twelfth century, when Hadrian[3], the English pope, made over Ireland to Henry II, that along with the English conquest the yoke of Roman dictation was firmly riveted on the neck of the ancient Irish Church.

This independence Columba brought with him to his new island-home off the west coast of Scotland. Iona became now the light of Christendom. For many generations it was the centre of the great evangelistic movements of the time. Not England or Scotland only, but large parts of the Continent also[4], were Christianized by these Irish missionaries, either from their adopted home in Iona or from their mother country.

And what of Northumbria meanwhile? Paulinus[5] had advanced northwards from the Roman mission in Kent; he had preached for a time to our pagan forefathers in Northumbria; but he had made no way. Disheartened by his patron's defeat and death, he abandoned the field, and retired southward to a more congenial sphere of work. The country remained pagan still. Not a single church, not a single altar, no symbol of the Gospel of any kind, we are told, had been erected between the Forth and the Tees[6]. For the Christian missionary it was virgin soil still. Then Iona stepped in, where Rome had failed. Some two years after the retreat of Paulinus, Aidan left the shores of Iona, and took up his abode at Lindisfarne. Oswald the king, educated as an exile in Iona, naturally sought thence the teacher who should win his newly-recovered kingdom for Christ. The story of Aidan's selection for the work is too well known to need repetition here. It is a noble testimony to the character of the man, his simplicity and his gentleness, his absolute self-renunciation and his unflinching faith. Never did the pure flame of the evangelistic spirit burn more brightly in any man. He had all the excellences of Columba, his melting sympathy, his fervid zeal, his directness of purpose. But we see none of the grave blots which sully the master's character—no irascibility, no vindictiveness, nothing of the headstrong and ungovernable passion. The capabilities of the Celtic temper were moulded and restrained by the spirit of Christ.

It was in the year 635—a little more than seventy years after Columba landed in Iona, just thirty years after the death of Augustine—that Aidan commenced his work. Though nearly forty years had elapsed since Augustine's first landing in England, Christianity was still confined to its first conquest, the south-east corner of the island, the kingdom of Kent. Beyond this border, though ground had been broken here and there, no territory had been permanently acquired for the Gospel. Then commenced those thirty years of earnest energetic labour, carried on by these Celtic missionaries and their disciples from Lindisfarne as their spiritual citadel, which ended in the submission of England to the gentle yoke of Christ. Not Augustine, but Aidan, is the true apostle of England.

Before I pass away from this Celtic period—the most attractive, and (in a spiritual aspect) the most splendid, in the annals of our Church—and proceed to speak of the Roman submission, let me dwell for a moment on the two great facts which this history reveals. These are the success of the Celtic preachers, and the independence of these Celtic missions.

1. Of the triumphs of the Celtic evangelists something has been said already. If we desire to know

the secret of their success, it is soon told. It was the power of earnest, simple, self-denying lives, pleading with a force which no eloquence of words can command. But whatever may be the explanation, the fact remains. Iona succeeded, where Rome had failed.

Lest I should seem to exaggerate or to heighten the colouring, I prefer to tell the tale not in my own language, but in words taken from an accomplished writer of the Roman Communion. 'From the cloisters of Lindisfarne,' writes Montalembert, 'and from the heart of those districts in which the popularity of ascetic pontiffs such as Aidan, and martyr kings such as Oswald and Oswin, took day by day a deeper root, Northumbrian Christianity spread over the southern kingdoms...What is distinctly visible is the influence of Celtic priests and missionaries everywhere replacing and seconding Roman missionaries, and reaching districts which their predecessors had never been able to enter. The stream of the Divine Word thus extended itself from north to south, and its slow but certain course reached in succession all the people of the Heptarchy[7].' And again, at the close of the chapters of which these are the opening words he writes; 'Of the eight kingdoms of the Anglo-Saxon Confederation, that of Kent alone was exclusively won and retained by the Roman monks, whose first attempts among the East Saxons and Northumbrians ended in failure. In Wessex and in East Anglia the Saxons of the West and the Angles of the East were converted by the combined action of continental missionaries and Celtic monks. As to the two Northumbrian kingdoms, and those of Essex and Mercia, which comprehended in themselves more than two-thirds of the territory occupied by the German conquerors, these four countries owed their final conversion exclusively to the peaceful invasion of the Celtic monks; who not only rivalled the zeal of the Roman monks, but who, the first obstacles once surmounted, shewed much more perseverance and gained much more success[8].' Sussex still remained heathen; Sussex, 'the smallest of all but one of the earliest founded[9];' Sussex, the immediate neighbour of the Roman missionaries in Kent. Sussex was at length stormed and taken. And here again the conqueror of this last stronghold of heathendom, though an ardent champion of the Roman cause, was a Northumbrian by birth. Wilfrid had been a pupil of Aidan, and his missionary inspiration was drawn from Lindisfarne. Was I not right then in claiming for Aidan the first place in the evangelisation of our race? Augustine was the apostle of Kent, but Aidan was the apostle of England.

2. The independence of the Celtic missionary again is a patent fact, and stands out in strong contrast to later evangelistic movements in Western

Europe. Rome neither initiated, nor controlled, these Celtic missions. The missionaries owed allegiance, not to the Bishop of Rome, but to the Presbyter-Abbot of Iona. There is no evidence that they sought or accepted any authoritative directions from the Roman mission in the south of England. Their usages were different in many respects from the usages of Rome. When these came under discussion, and it was a question between allegiance to Iona and allegiance to Rome, they unhesitatingly chose the former. It is probable, indeed, that if asked they would have granted a certain precedency to the great patriarch of the West, the bishop of the world's metropolis, though of this there is no evidence; but it is quite plain on the other hand that in their eyes he had no constitutional right to command them. Roman direction is treated as absolutely valueless by them; Roman wishes are disregarded. Sooner than abandon the traditions and customs of Iona for those of Rome, they retire altogether from the field, leaving the rich fruits of their labours to others at the very moment when the harvest is full ripe. The Abbot of Iona—the successor of Columba—is their acknowledged ruler, the ruler even of bishops, though only a simple presbyter, their superior in ecclesiastical office, though their inferior in spiritual functions[10]. From him they receive their commission, though not their consecration; and to him they render their account. The bishop of Rome is in no sense their master.

But this Celtic period was brought suddenly to a close. The rivalry between Rome and Iona came to a head. The dispute was about matters unimportant in themselves[11]. There was the cut of the tonsure, a wholly trivial matter, in which there could not be a right or a wrong. There was the time of the Easter celebration, which was a question of convenience rather than principle. The real issue lay behind all these petty disputes. It was the alternative of allegiance to Rome or allegiance to Iona. The conference was held at Whitby[12]. On the side of Iona were all the great makers of England. Hilda the royal abbess, Colman the successor of Aidan, Cedd the great missionary bishop. But the fiat of the king prevailed. Iona was defeated. The Celtic brotherhood at Lindisfarne was broken up. Colman retired with the brothers and their scholars to their Scottish home. 'What heart,' writes Montalembert, 'is so cold as not to understand, to sympathise, and to journey with him, along the Northumbrian coast and over the Scottish mountains, where, bearing homeward the bones of his father [Aidan], the proud but vanquished spirit returned to his northern mists, and buried in the sacred isle of Iona his defeat and his unconquerable fidelity to the traditions of his race?'[13]

To the English Churchman the event will suggest other and wider reflexions beside.

So the Celtic missionaries laboured, and others were to enter into their labours. Once again the saying was fulfilled, 'One soweth and another reapeth.' But an irreparable loss was inflicted on the English Church by the withdrawal of this child-like simplicity, this generous devotion, this fervour of missionary zeal. Devout and upright men, like Bede[14], even though their sympathies might be with Rome in the dispute, yet writing while the memory of these Celtic days was fresh, looked back with longing eyes on the departed glory. It was the golden age of saintliness, such as England would never see again.

Yet along with this terrible loss the change brought some great and immediate practical advantages. To be united with Rome was to be connected with the centre of the highest Christian civilisation and art of the age. What the rude Celtic churches with their walls of timber and their thatch of reeds were to the stone buildings of the 'Roman' style, as Bede calls it[15], introduced by Benedict Biscop from the Continent, this the civilisation of Iona was to the civilisation of Rome. Moreover, Christian Rome had inherited from heathen Rome her great capacity for organisation; and just here lay the main defect of the Celtic Churches. The Celtic Churches of Ireland remained without regular parochial and diocesan organisation for many centuries later. Still the English subjugation brought with it the Roman ascendancy. The English soil was more favourable than the native Irish for organisation, and accordingly the Celtic Church of Northumbria fared better. But organisation was still its great want. Thus the connexion with Rome supplied the element of progress which at this moment the Celtic Churches most needed. Moreover, the Roman submission brought one other paramount advantage. The development of England demanded unity, but unity there was not. Politically, the island was broken up into several independent kingdoms. Ecclesiastically, there were two independent Churches, the Celtic in the North, the Roman in the South. The unity of the Church was the first step towards the unity of the State. At whatever cost this unity was attained at Whitby, and the State soon followed in the wake of the Church.

These immediate advantages were so tangible and so patent that it is no surprise to find men like Benedict Biscop and Chad and Bede welcoming the Roman submission. The tremendous ulterior consequences were quite beyond the range of human foresight.

Nor must we forget that the submission required by Gregory and his immediate successors was different in kind from the imperious demands of Rome in a later age. Two centuries were yet to elapse before the forgery of the False Decretals[16] furnished a documentary basis for the claims of Rome. In exalting the power of the Roman See Gregory exerted a practical influence second to none of his predecessors; he strained the authority of the patriarchal chair to the utmost; he was far from consistent in his language. But at least he denounces[17] the title of 'Universal Bishop' as a proud and pestilent assumption, an act of contempt and wrong to the whole priesthood, an imitation of Satan, who exalted himself above his fellow angels, a token of the speedy coming of antichrist.

Thus passes away 'this goodliest fellowship' 'whereof the world holds record[18].' Of these splendid traditions, of this bright example, of these evangelistic triumphs, you are the heirs. This diocese of Newcastle still enshrines the Holy Island of Lindisfarne, the true cradle of English Christianity. The building, whose completion and adornment we this day celebrate, is in some sense a replacement of the older sanctuary. If it is ever to fulfil its mission it will become not only the house of more ornate and frequent services, of a more splendid ritual, but before all things the centre of intense missionary and philanthropic work. After all it was not the splendour, but the simplicity, of Iona and of Lindisfarne, that won England for Christ. Times are changed. The evangelistic agencies of that age were modelled on the monastic type. None other, so far as we can see, would then have done the work so well. Times are changed. No one could wish now to replace the stately pile of William of Carileph by the wooden shed of Finan[19]. Art, music, poetry, architecture, all the choicest adornments of life which God has given us, these we are bound to render to the service of the sanctuary, not selfishly keeping our best for our private homes. But while all else changes, the spirit is unchanged. The simplicity, the self-devotion, the prayerfulness, the burning love of Christ, which shone forth in those Celtic missionaries of old, must be your spiritual equipment now. Then, when your work is done, and another generation shall have taken your place, it may be that some future Bede will again trace in words of tender and regretful sympathy the undying record of a Christ-like life and work.

S. OSWALD.

PREACHED IN S. OSWALD'S, DURHAM, AT THE RE-OPENING OF THE CHURCH.

August 1, 1883.

Like unto him was there no king before him, that turned to the Lord with all his heart, and with all his soul, and with all his might.

2 KINGS xxiii. 25.

Kings shall be thy nursing fathers.

ISAIAH xlix. 23.

WHAT have been the relations of the Church of God to the kings and rulers of this world in different ages? What has been the influence of those relations on its immediate work and on its permanent well-being? How far has it gained or lost by the support or the opposition of the civil power? What strength, what weakness, what education, what corruptions, can be traced to its alliance or its antagonisms with the State or the chiefs of the State? These are questions of momentous interest at all times, but never more so than at the present season.

One signal crisis in the history of God's people, when the alliance between Church and State, between king and priest, was most close, is the reign of that Jewish sovereign whose praises I have just quoted from the record of the Books of Kings. Alike in the reformation of religion and in the disasters which followed, the grasp of the temporal power held the Church tight, so that for good or for evil the destiny of the one was involved in the destiny of the other. David, Hezekiah, Josiah, these three are singled out by the Son of Sirach[20] as alone not defective in the long list of Jewish kings. All the rest 'forsook the law of the Most High.' But of the three thus excepted Josiah was the most steadfast, the most earnest, the most courageous champion of religion and protector of the Church.

The Old Testament records no more tragic career—as men count tragic—than the history of Josiah. A period of gross and flagrant apostasy has preceded. His grandfather Manasseh and his father Amon take their rank among the basest renegades of the Jewish sovereignty. Manasseh indeed repents, but Amon dies impenitent. 'Amon,' we are told, 'trespassed more and more.' Idolatry was rampant everywhere. The worship of Baal and Ashtoreth, of Chemosh and Milcom, all the cruelties and all the profligacies which accompanied the foul rites of the gods of the heathen, ran riot in the land. Amon was murdered by his subjects. Josiah, then a young child, succeeded to this inheritance of corruption and disorder. At once everything is changed. The young king 'walked in all the ways of David his father, and turned not aside to the right hand or to the left.' The book of the law was rediscovered. The covenant with God was renewed. The land was swept clean of its idolatry and its abominations—clean 'as a man wipeth a dish, wiping it and turning it upside down.' The restoration of religion culminated in a great celebration of the chief national and religious festival, a celebration which was renowned through after-ages. 'There was not holden such a passover from the days of the judges that judged Israel, nor in all the days of the kings of Israel, nor of the kings of Judah.' What testimony more complete could we desire to the fervour, the devotion, the severe conscientiousness of this king, whose fidelity to the God of Abraham gilded the eventide of the kingdom with a parting glory, ere it set in darkness? Might not the sacred chronicler with justice record that 'like unto him was there no king before him... neither after him arose there any like him?[21]'

Yet the next recorded incident is that he was cut off prematurely, cut off suddenly, cut off in his mid-career of pious service to Jehovah, cut off by a heathen king at the head of a heathen host. This was the beginning of the end. When Josiah was lost, all was lost. Therefore we are told 'All Judah and Jerusalem mourned for Josiah.' The mourning of Hadad-rimmon[22] became henceforth the type and proverb of a great national grief. Megiddo was a household word for a mighty overthrow. Where else should the Apocalyptic seer[23] place the great and final conflict, when the powers of Satan should muster against the armies of the Lord, but in this great scene of conflict and agony, in Armageddon, the 'Hill of Megiddo'? For many generations the day of Josiah's death was kept as a day of mourning by the nation. 'All the singing men and the singing women spake of Josiah in their lamentations to this day, and made them an ordinance in Israel.' Had not the men of that generation just cause to complain that the fathers had eaten sour grapes, and the children's teeth were set on edge? Manasseh and Amon had sown the wind, and Josiah must reap the whirlwind.

Analogies have not unnaturally been sought to the person and history of Josiah in sovereigns of later ages. The reign of our sixth Edward lent itself easily to such an application. The youth of the king, the reformation of religion, these two facts combined were enough to suggest the parallel. In both cases also the sovereigns came to an untimely end. But here the resemblance ceased. There was only a sharp contrast between the wasting away of the boy-king before he had attained his sixteenth year on a lingering sick-bed, and the mortal wound which carried off the Jewish monarch in the prime of mature age on the battle-field.

A truer parallel might be found in the great Northumbrian king, whose name is borne by this church, and whose memory we are bound this day to celebrate. Listen to these words: 'The remembrance of Oswald is sweet as honey in all mouths, and as music in a banquet of wine. He behaved himself uprightly in the conversion of the people, and took away the abominations of idolatry. He directed his heart unto the Lord, and in the time of the ungodly he established the worship of God.' Might we not imagine that we had here the language of Bede or Adamnan describing the hero-saint of Northumbria? Yet the passage which I have quoted is taken word for word from Ecclesiasticus[24], with only the substitution of a name, Oswald for Josiah.

Like the Jewish king, Oswald succeeded to the throne after a period of apostasy. The year immediately preceding was the darkest in the annals of Northumbrian Christendom. The two kings of Northumbria, Osric of Deira and Eanfrid of Bernicia, renounced the faith of Christ, in which they had been brought up. Osric was the cousin, and Eanfrid the brother, of Oswald[25]. Thus Oswald, like Josiah, succeeded to a heritage of apostasy, bequeathed to him by his own blood-relations. In after-ages this dark year was not reckoned by the names of the perfidious sovereigns, but added, so Bede tells us[26], to the reign of their successor, 'Oswald, the man beloved of God.' The apostasy of the Northumbrian kings was not the only calamity which overwhelmed the Church. The Northumbrian prelate Paulinus had deserted his post, and found refuge in the South. 'This ill-omened year,' says Bede[27], 'remains to this day hateful to all good men.' The Church was disorganised, desolated, almost pulverised. It seemed as if Christianity would be stamped out in these northern kingdoms.

Like Josiah, Oswald came as a restorer. From the first moment he never hesitated. He took up his position as a Christian, and he consistently, bravely, faithfully maintained it to his last breath, reckless of all consequences to himself. He rebuilt the ruined walls of the spiritual Jerusalem. He re-created the Church of Northumbria; and after a reign of eight short years he left it so strong that it had little or nothing to fear from the powers of this world.

But if Oswald's career resembled Josiah's in the heritage to which he succeeded, if the Northumbrian sovereign was the counterpart to the Jewish in the main work of his reign, and in the resolute spirit which animated this work, still more striking is the similarity in the circumstances of their death. Both died at about the same age, the age which has proved fatal to the lives of so many famous men,—the thirty-eighth or thirty-ninth year. Both received their death-wound in battle. Both died in the moment of defeat, leaving the pagans victorious on the field, and bequeathing sorrow to the Church of God, for which they had fought and conquered, had lived and died.

The reign of Oswald, his whole public career so far as we know, eight years in all, begins and ends with a battle. For a just estimate of his motives, his character, and his worth, we have no better preparation than a review of these two scenes of battle.

The scene of the first battle[28] is the neighbourhood of Hexham, under the shelter of the Roman wall, the spot marked in after-ages by the Chapel of S. Oswald. The apostate kings have been slain in battle. Oswald, baptized and educated as a Christian in Scotland, comes to claim his inheritance, comes as the champion of the Church of Christ. He is met by the forces of the British warrior Cadwalla, the ally of the heathen Penda, the Mercian king. The battle is imminent. A wooden cross is hastily constructed; a hole is dug in the ground; the king seizes the cross, and plants it in the earth, holds it with either hand, while the soldiers fill in the soil. Then he cries aloud to his assembled troops, 'Let us all fall on our knees, and together supplicate the Lord Omnipotent, the living and the true, that of His mercy He will defend us from a proud and fierce enemy; for He knoweth that we have undertaken a righteous war for the salvation of our race.' He was obeyed. This done, at dawn of day the soldiers advanced against the enemy. Their armies were crowned with victory, and Cadwalla—the hero of forty battles and sixty skirmishes—was slain. The name of the place, Heavenfield, seemed after the event to have had a prophetic import. Once again the visible cross had been the standard of victory. Once again the watchword of the Christian warrior had been *Hoc signo vinces*; but a purer, nobler, simpler, manlier heart beat in Oswald's breast than in Constantine's.

The second battle-field[20] is a pathetic contrast to the first. The enemy here is the heathen king, the Mercian Penda, the old ally of Cadwalla. The scene of battle is called Maserfield, commonly identified with Oswestry—Oswald's Tree, Oswald's Cross, as it was designated by the Britons. The pagan was victorious, Oswald was surrounded by the enemy, and slain on the field. His dying words, a prayer for his soldiers, passed into a proverb, 'O God, have mercy on their souls, said Oswald falling to the ground.' What wonder that in after-times the grass seemed to grow more green on the spot where he fell, that the very dust gathered from the ground was thought to be endowed with miraculous virtues? The day of his earthly death, the day of his heavenly birth, was August the fifth. Year by year, as the season recurred, the monks of Hexham repaired to the scene of his first battle, there with solemn service to celebrate the anniversary of his last. Thus Oswald's earliest cross was linked with his latest.

It is the special privilege of a bishop of Durham that he is surrounded on all sides with the memorials of an early Christendom. Just a fortnight ago I took occasion at the millenary festival of the church of Chester-le-Street to speak of the lessons bequeathed to us by the character and destiny of Cuthbert. My work to-day is a fit sequel to the former task. In the conventional representations of sculpture Cuthbert's mitred figure bears in his hands Oswald's crowned head. Oswald's skull was enclosed in Cuthbert's coffin. Oswald's parish church looks across the Wear on Cuthbert's great cathedral. The same man, William of Carileph, was, I believe, the builder both of the one and of the other. Having then spoken so lately of Cuthbert, how can I do otherwise than speak of Oswald to-day?

The Church is built on the foundation of the apostles and prophets; but the upper layers of the masonry are the words and works, the lives and deaths, of the saints and martyrs and evangelists and teachers of succeeding ages. The past has much to teach us, if we approach it with reverence. Contempt would only blind our eyes. In many things we see further, much further, than Aidan and Oswald and Cuthbert. Strange, if it were otherwise. But what ground for self-complacency is there here? The dwarf on the giant's shoulders has a wider range of vision than the giant. Our seat of vantage is a giant Christendom of eighteen centuries. But let us not deceive ourselves. Reverence is not slavery. We may admire the zeal and devotion, the simplicity and the faith, without acquiescing in the ignorance or embracing the superstition, of the past. We have need even when we are scanning the saintliest lives to prove the spirits, that we may choose the good and reject the evil.

What then are the lessons which Oswald has bequeathed to us? What has he done for us, which demands our thanksgiving to-day? What was there in the character, the life, the work of the man, of permanent value for us all?

1. I would ask you first to consider our obligations to him as the pioneer of the Gospel in these parts. He is the one human agent to whom more than to any other we in these regions owe our

Christianity. I spoke of him before, as having re-created the Church of Northumbria. But in the northern of the two Northumbrian kingdoms, the Church can hardly be said to have existed before his time. Bede says distinctly that 'no sign of the Christian faith, no church, no altar, had ever been erected throughout the nation of the Bernicians' before Oswald planted the cross on his first battle-field. Nor was he content with the erection of external symbols. He took immediate steps for the instruction of the people. Not from Rome, but from Iona, he invited his evangelists. He himself related[30] how on the eve of the battle of Heavenfield the saintly founder of Iona, Columba, the apostle of the North, appeared to him in angelic form and shining raiment, bidding him, 'Be of good courage and play the man.' Hence it came to pass that the evangelisation of these northern counties flowed almost solely from Celtic, and not Roman sources. In the simple, wise, sympathetic, large-hearted, saintly Aidan, to whom Northumbria owes its conversion, we have an evangelist of the purest and noblest type. Hardly a single incident is recorded of him, which we could wish untrue; and there are very few Christian saints and heroes in any age, of whom so much can be said. I know not how it is that when so many recent churches bear the names of Cuthbert and Oswald and Bede, Aidan has been almost overlooked in our modern dedications. Yet to whom do we owe more than to him? And Oswald gave us Aidan.

2. But secondly; we trace back to Oswald the earliest alliance of Church and State in these parts. In the fullest and best sense Oswald was a 'nursing father' to the Church. Oswald and Aidan worked hand in hand together. Aidan preached, and Oswald interpreted. As Moses and Aaron together led the chosen people through the wilderness unto the land of promise, as Zerubbabel the son of Shealtiel and Joshua the son of Josedech worked together in repairing the walls of the Holy City and in building the House of God, so Oswald the king and Aidan the bishop laboured with one mind and one soul for the ingathering of the wanderers and the erection of the spiritual temple. It is not my business now to consider under what circumstances the disadvantages may outweigh the advantages of a close alliance between the spiritual and the temporal power. But the ideal at least is an absolute union between the one and the other, so that the kingdom of this world may be the kingdom of Christ. And in those rude ages under sovereigns like Oswald, who can doubt that the spread of the Gospel and the consolidation of the Church gained enormously by the alliance?

3. But again; our thanksgiving is due also for

the personal character of the king. Nursing fathers of the Church have not always led the saintliest lives. The character of Constantine will not bear very close inspection. Even rapacity and greed and selfishness may by God's good providence be used as instruments of religious reform or spiritual advancement. But there is always some loss in such cases. It was said by a famous heathen writer of old[31] that states would then be governed perfectly when kings were philosophers, and philosophers were kings. We may fitly adopt and modify this saying. In the Christian ideal of human society kings should be saints, and saints should be kings. The combination is rare. As we have had kings who were not saints, so also we have had saints on the throne who were not kings. Edward the Confessor and Henry the Sixth were in some sense saints, but they were deficient in kingly qualities. On the other hand, in Alfred of England and S. Louis of France the king and the saint are combined. In this small class of kingly saints and saintly kings Oswald takes his rank. He was every whit a king. In a short reign of eight years he placed Northumbria once more united and organised at the head of the kingdoms of the Heptarchy. He himself became the chosen suzerain of the whole English people. But he was not less a saint. He was profuse in almsgiving; he spent whole hours during the night in prayer. His first and his last recorded public utterances, as we have seen, were prayers. A cross began and a cross ended his reign.

4. And this brings me to speak of the fourth and last lesson which I desire to draw from Oswald's career. The end of Oswald's life, like the end of Josiah's, was an outrage on poetic justice. But God's ways are not our ways. The defeat and slaughter of men like Josiah and Oswald is a voice from God declaring in emphatic tones to those who have ears to hear that death is not the end of all things; that this life is only the germ of the true life; that the fleeting 'now' is as nothing to the never-ending hereafter. What is the momentary death-pang, what is the transient disaster, when brought face to face with eternal being? Their mortal bodies might die; but their work could not die; they themselves could not die. The anniversary of Josiah's death was celebrated by loud wailing and national lamentation. On the anniversary of Oswald's death thanks were given to Almighty God 'for the gladsome and holy rejoicing of this day'—I am quoting the words of the old collect[32]. Whence this difference? Is it not that Christ's passion and resurrection have shed a glory over death, as the portal of eternity? Christ brought life and immortality to light. After all was the cross of

suffering at Oswestry so unfit a sequel to the cross of self-dedication at Heavenfield?

Lord, teach us this lesson of Oswald's life, of Oswald's death; teach us always in joy and in sorrow, in success and in adversity, in victory and in defeat, to bear Thy cross now, that we may wear Thy crown hereafter.

S. AIDAN.

PREACHED AT THE CONSECRATION OF S. AIDAN'S
CHURCH, BLACKHILL.

December 7, 1883.

The glory of children are their fathers.
PROVERBS xvii. 6.

'AT this time there befell a great slaughter, none greater in the Church or nation of the Northumbrians.'

This is the language of Bede[83], describing the disastrous defeat at the battle of Hatfield in 633—a great crisis in the history not of Northumbria only, but of England. It seemed for the moment as if the unity and the evangelisation of England were indefinitely postponed. Of the allied chieftains who dealt the fatal blow, the one the Mercian Penda[34], a pagan still, was an enemy by religion, the other the British sovereign Cadwalla, though professedly a Christian, yet only in semblance a friend by creed, was an enemy by race. The Northumbrian king Edwin was slain; neither age nor sex was spared; Christianity was stamped out.

Only six years before this date Edwin had avowed

himself a convert to Christianity. The Roman missionary Paulinus, consecrated bishop by a successor of S. Augustine of Canterbury, had accompanied Edwin's bride, the Christian princess Ethelburga of Kent, as her chaplain, when she settled in her northern home. He had preached far and wide; he had baptized whole multitudes; he seemed to be carrying everything before him. The conversion of a king in those days was the natural prelude to the conversion of his subjects. The name Pallinsbourne on the Scottish frontier still bears testimony to the energy and success of the preacher. Meanwhile the civil and political condition of the people was not less satisfactory. From the Forth to the Humber Edwin reigned over an undivided Northumbrian kingdom. His name and power have left behind them an imperishable memorial in the royal city of Edinburgh. But his authority extended far beyond the limits of his own kingdom. He was acknowledged as sovereign lord in the other kingdoms of the Heptarchy. It was the first time that any English prince had held this proud position. His kingdom was reaping the fruits of a strong and settled government. It was remarked that now first a woman with a babe in her arms might have wandered from sea to sea without fear of molestation[35].

By the defeat at Hatfield all was changed. The

Northumbrian kingdom was broken up again into two provinces. The two rulers were worse than pagans; they were apostates. They succumbed speedily to a foreign invader. It was the darkest year in the annals of Northumbria. Everywhere was dissolution, anarchy, ruin. The supremacy of Northumbria in the Heptarchy was gone. The hasty and superficial work of Paulinus had come to nought. He himself bowed before the storm, abandoned these northern kingdoms, and sought a more tranquil sphere of labour in the South. The night of heathendom again closed over the land. The first chapter in the history of Northumbrian Christianity was ended. The Roman mission, despite all the feverish energy of its chief, had proved a failure. A sponge had passed over Northumbria, and scarce a vestige of his work remained.

It was not from imperial Rome, nor from Kent, the handmaid of Rome, that Northumbria was destined to receive her Christianity. A larger and freer spirit must be stamped on the English Church in her infancy, never to be obliterated in maturer age. The cradle of Northumbrian Christianity was a bleak, lonely island off the western coast of Scotland. Here, just seventy years before the epoch of which I am speaking, the tender, passionate, remorseful, sympathetic Irishman, Columba—a Celt of the Celts—had settled; and under his fostering care a religious house had sprung up, the nursery of saints and scholars, who were to carry the faith of Christ and the light of learning far beyond the boundaries of the British Isles, beyond even the lofty mountain barrier of the Alps, invading Italy itself with a peaceful invasion. To this sanctuary of religion the Northumbrian prince Oswald had fled as a young lad on his father's death. There under the immediate successors of Columba he was reared and taught the faith of Christ. Thence he issued, a young man not yet thirty, to recover his hereditary kingdom. The light of dawn broke on the dark fatal year of Northumbrian annals. His arms were crowned with triumph. The cross was once more planted in Northumbrian soil. The whole kingdom was again united under the sway of one prince.

At this point begins the true history of Northumbrian Christianity. When Oswald planted the cross under the shadow of the old Roman wall on the site of his earliest battle-field, we are expressly told that it was the first erected in the northern of the two Northumbrian kingdoms, which extended from the Forth to the Tees. So entirely had the whirlwind sweeping over the land obliterated the footprints of Paulinus.

The cross planted by Oswald on the battle-field, and the victory achieved thereupon, were only the type of the spiritual efforts and the spiritual conquests which were to follow. Not content with fixing the outward symbol of man's redemption in his native soil, he would plant the cross of Christ in the hearts of his people. To Iona, the home of his own spiritual nurture, he betook himself for aid. The response was worthy of the appeal. Just twelve centuries and a half ago, in the year 635, Aidan, consecrated bishop, left the shores of Iona, and fixed his head-quarters in Lindisfarne, the Holy Island of the eastern coast, almost beneath the shadow of the rock fortress of Bamborough, the residence of the Northumbrian kings.

I may be pardoned this day, if I tell once again the oft-repeated tale of Aidan's selection for the office[36]. He was not the first choice of his spiritual superiors for this arduous work. The first missionary sent out from Iona had failed signally, even more signally than the Roman Paulinus. He returned speedily to Iona disheartened, reporting that these Northumbrians were a stubborn and impracticable people, with whom nothing could be done. Aidan was present at this conference. He broke in, 'Brother, it seems to me that thou hast been unduly hard upon these untaught hearers, and hast not given them first according to the Apostle's precept the milk of less solid doctrine, until gradually nurtured on the Word of God they should have strength enough to digest the more perfect lessons.' All eyes were turned upon the speaker. Here was the very man whom the work demanded. The humility, the patience, the gentle sympathy, the wise discretion, the whole character of the man flashes out in this simple, eager utterance.

I know no nobler type of the missionary spirit than Aidan. His character, as it appears through the haze of antiquity, is almost absolutely faultless. Doubtless this haze may have obscured some imperfections which a clearer atmosphere and a nearer view would have enabled us to detect. But we cannot have been misled as to the main lineaments of the man. Measuring him side by side with other great missionaries of those days, Augustine of Canterbury, or Wilfrid of York, or Cuthbert of his own Lindisfarne, we are struck with the singular sweetness and breadth and sympathy of his character. He had all the virtues of his Celtic race without any of its faults. A comparison with his own spiritual forefather—the eager, headstrong, irascible, affectionate, penitent, patriotic, self-devoted Columba, the most romantic and attractive of all early medieval saints—will justify this sentiment. He was tender, sympathetic, adventurous, self-sacrificing; but he was patient, steadfast, calm, appreciative, discreet before all things. 'This grace of discretion,' writes Bede[37], 'marked him out for the Northumbrian mission; but when the time came he was found to be adorned with every other excellence.' This ancient historian never tires of his theme, when he is praising Aidan. 'He was a man,' he writes, 'of surpassing gentleness, and piety and self-restraint.' Among other traits of a holy life 'he left to the clergy a most wholesome example of abstinence and continence.' 'He lived among his friends none otherwise than he taught.' 'He cared not to seek anything, to love anything, belonging to this world.' He was incessant in his journeys through town and country, always travelling on foot where it was possible. Those who accompanied him on his walks were expected to occupy themselves in reading the scriptures or learning the psalms; 'a strange contrast,' adds Bede, 'to the slothfulness of our own age.' He redeemed many captives, and educated them when redeemed for the priesthood. He rebuked the misdemeanours of the wealthy without fear or favour. He was most merciful and kindly to the poor, a very father to the wretched. On one occasion king Oswyn had given him a fine horse, suitably caparisoned, to carry him on his frequent journeys through field and flood. A poor man came in his way and asked an alms. He dismounted and gave the horse to his petitioner. The king, hearing of this, remonstrated: 'Were there not poorer horses, or other less costly gifts, to bestow upon a beggar?' His reply combines the quick repartee of the Irishman with the earnestness of a devout Christian soul, 'What sayest thou, king? Is yon son of a mare more precious in thy sight than yon son of God?[38]' The secret of his power reveals itself in this rejoinder. He treated all men, even the lowliest, not only with sympathy as brothers, but with reverence as sons of God.

We may confidently accept everything that Bede tells us in praise of S. Aidan. The channels through which the information has passed were not too partial to the theme of their eulogy. Roman supremacy prevailed before Bede wrote. Aidan had not acknowledged this foreign allegiance. He owed obedience, not to Rome, but to Iona. Along with his spiritual fathers and brothers, he accepted the rule of S. Columba, and he rejected Roman usages. This was a grave offence with Bede's contemporaries. In Bede's language Aidan's was a zeal for God, but not according to knowledge. But Bede was a truthful and a kindly man, and he could not withhold the rich tribute of admiration due to the apostolic zeal and simplicity of the evangelist of Northumbria.

Do we wonder that a character so deep and yet so attractive drew men after it with the cords of power and of love? Daily, we are told, recruits came in from the West, and 'preached the word of faith with great devotion.' Churches were built; crowds of people flocked to hear the message; lands were given for religious purposes; monasteries and schools were built, where English children were taught by Celtic missionaries from Ireland and from the Scotch coast.

Aidan was both a diligent student and an assiduous teacher. He would not have been true to his spiritual nurture otherwise. Iona was at this time the focus of intellectual light to Western Christendom. It is a curious fact that the great crisis in Columba's life is said to have been a quarrel for the possession of a book—the Battle of the Psalter—when the blood shed through his means filled his soul with penitential remorse and drove him to perpetual exile in Iona, there to atone for the slaughter of bodies by the conversion of souls. Aidan saw that if the foundations of the Church were to be solidly laid, education must be a chief part of his work. He gathered about him a class of the most promising lads, twelve in number, many of them famous in after-life. He seems to have had a remarkable insight into character. The same appreciation, which led him to recall Hilda to his side for an important work, would guide him in the selection of his pupils. Among the members of his class were Eata, his successor in the see of Lindisfarne, and the two brothers Chad and Cedd[39], the evangelists of southern England; and Wilfrid, the most famous of northern Churchmen in the succeeding age.

Aidan was the intimate friend and counsellor of two successive Northumbrian sovereigns. This close alliance of king and bishop contributed largely to the progress and the evangelisation of England. Of these two sovereigns, the first, Oswald, immediately on his accession had brought him from his northern home to take charge of the mission; the death of the second, Oswyn, preceded his own by a few days. Thus his episcopate was co-extensive with the two reigns.

The death of Oswyn was a fatal blow to him. Twelve days later, leaning against a wooden buttress at the west end of the church of Bamborough he breathed out his soul, on the last day of August 651. The day is fitly designated in the Calendars, 'Aidan's Rest,' *Quies Aidani*. It was a tranquil close to a tranquil life; most tranquil within, but most laborious without.

Once again, as he mentions his death, laying aside his Roman partialities, Bede turns aside to pay his parting tribute of respect to so much worth. Though not approving his Easter usage, he feels himself constrained, he tells us, as a truthful historian to praise what deserves praise, his diligent pursuit of peace and love, of chastity and humility; his spirit superior to avarice, and contemptuous of pride and vain-glory; his assiduity in doing and teaching the heavenly precepts; his industry in reading and in vigils; his resoluteness, alike in condemning the proud and powerful, and in comforting the feeble, in relieving the poor and upholding clemency. 'In short,' he adds[40], 'he was careful not to neglect any duty which he had learnt from the writings of the evangelists and apostles and prophets, but to put every one in practice with all his might. These features,' he continues, 'I heartily cherish and love, because I believe them to be well-pleasing to God.'

Is not the memory of such a man—the truest of saints and the greatest of benefactors—an undeserved inheritance which we too are bound to cherish with affectionate reverence? Yet, while S. Cuthbert has been honoured with memorials far and wide, not a single church, so far as I remember, has been dedicated to S. Aidan within this county of Durham in ancient or modern times. This neglect is not difficult to explain. His divergence from the Roman usage was a fatal barrier to a just recognition, while Rome gave the law to Western Christendom; and the precedent thus set prevailed, even when Roman ascendancy had passed away.

Aidan was succeeded by Finan, a man likeminded with himself; and Finan by Colman. Both alike came, as he had come, from the parent monastery of Iona. Both alike adhered, as he had adhered, to the usages of S. Columba. The three episcopates together covered a period of thirty years. Then came a change. At the synod of Whitby, despite Colman and Hilda, the use of Rome prevailed over the use of Iona by the influence of the king. Colman, the last of the Celtic bishops, retired with a large band of followers from Northumbria. A new volume in the history of the Northumbrian Church was opened, with the impress of Rome upon its pages. The age of Oswald and Aidan and Hilda was past.

This was the first rivet of the Roman yoke, which was to press so heavily on England in the generations to come. Yet it would be foolish to ignore the immediate advantages of this submission. The Church of England needed unity before all things. But this was impossible, while there was one Church in the North looking to Iona for guidance, and another in the South owing allegiance to Rome. Moreover, the fuller development of the English Church required that it should be drawn into the main stream of Christian civilisation, which at this time flowed through Rome. While we are thankful that the foundations of our Northumbrian Church were laid on the simplicity and devotion, the free spirit, the tenderness and love, the apostolic zeal of the missionaries of Iona, we need not shrink from acknowledging that she learnt much from the more complete organisation and the higher culture, of which Rome was then the schoolmistress.

Nor may we forget that the claims of Rome in this early age were modest indeed compared with her later assumptions. It is an enormous stride from the supremacy of Gregory the Great, as the patriarch of the West and the father of the English Church in the sixth century, to the practical despotism claimed by Hildebrand and Innocent III in the eleventh and succeeding centuries, as it is again a still vaster stride from the latter to the absolute infallibility asserted by Pius IX in the nineteenth century. Was it not Gregory the Great himself who denounced the title of 'Universal Bishop' as a blasphemy against God, who declared that in arrogating this title the Patriarch of Constantinople treated the whole episcopal order with contempt, and who maintained that the Apostles themselves—even Peter, the chief of the Apostles—though heads of their own particular branches, were only members of the universal Church?

Our act of dedication this day is a tribute to a memory which ought to be very sacred to us all. Nor will it stand alone. Already one new parish on the south, and another on the north, of the Tyne have been created, bearing this same honoured name[41]. The cloud which so long has obscured the renown of this saintliest of saints and truest of evangelists is passing away. 'The glory of children are their fathers.' We English Churchmen have a spiritual ancestry great and glorious, such as few Churches can boast. Of all the famous names of saintly heroes of the past, none shines with a brighter or more heavenly lustre than Aidan, the founder of the family. Pouring out our thanksgiving to God to-day, we will remember the debt which we owe to His faithful servant who claims our homage.

There is first the most obvious obligation to him as our first evangelist. He laid the foundations of the Northumbrian Church deep and strong. In sixteen years he accomplished for Northumbria and for England a work, which in less devoted hands might have demanded the labours of many generations.

Secondly, he is a true type and symbol of the freedom of the Church of England. Through the long ages of Roman domination the English Church was the least enslaved of all the Churches. Her statute-book is a continued protest against this foreign aggression. Her ablest kings were the resolute opponents of Roman usurpation. When the yoke was finally thrown off, though the strong will of the reigning sovereign was the active agent, yet it was the independent spirit of the clergy and people which rendered the change possible. Hence there was no break in the continuity of the English Church. Of this independent spirit which culminated in the Reformation, Aidan, our spiritual forefather, as we have seen, was the earliest embodiment.

And our thanksgivings are due not less for the splendour of a great pattern. No example is so potent as the example of a famous ancestry. It is a strength and an inspiration to their descendants. The fine old maxim reminds us that nobility obliges. The baseness of degenerate sons becomes all the more base by contrast with the worth of their fathers. You have acknowledged the obligation to-day by the dedication of this church. Henceforward Aidan's name and example will be ever before you. Year by year you will hold your parish festival; and what fitter time can you select for this purpose than the last day of August—the anniversary of 'Aidan's rest'? Thus year by year the lesson will be set vividly before your eyes. On this bright joyful day, when months of labour and anxiety are crowned by the consecration of your church, what better prayer can I offer for you, and you for yourselves, than that you all—clergy and laity alike—may tread in the footsteps, and be animated by the spirit, of Aidan your saintly forefather? With your larger opportunities, and your wider intellectual range, what may you not achieve, if you reproduce in your lives the humility, the holiness, the unbounded self-devotion, the unfailing sympathy and love, of this ancient servant of God? Believe it ; 'the glory of the children are their fathers.'

S. HILDA.

PREACHED AT THE CONSECRATION OF S. PAUL'S CHURCH, WEST HARTLEPOOL.

November 18, 1885.

I arose, a mother in Israel.
JUDGES v. 7.

THE period of Israelite history comprised in the Book of Judges is briefly summed up in one expressive sentence; 'Every man did that which was right in his own eyes.' It was a period of disorganisation and tumult. A judge arose in this place or in that. He was acknowledged by one tribe and repudiated by another. The nation was exposed to repeated and disastrous attacks from the surrounding peoples. There was no central authority at home. Again and again Israel lay at the mercy of her enemies; again and again by an unforeseen deliverance the nation was saved from extinction. It was a unique chapter in the world's history—this career of the Jewish people, 'persecuted but not forsaken,' 'chastened but not killed,' 'dying, and behold it lived.'

An eventful moment had arrived in this critical epoch when the words of the text were spoken. The enemy were pressing hard upon the chosen people. Their counsels were paralysed by the apathy of despair. They could only hang their hands and await their fate. Suddenly a woman's voice was heard amidst the confusion and dismay. A woman's hand was raised to wave them forward to battle. She —Deborah—arose, a mother in Israel. The foe was vanquished; the terror passed away; the sunlight broke once more through the darkness. A fresh lease of life was granted to the nation.

This prominence of a woman guiding the destinies of the people has, so far as I remember, no parallel in the great classical nations of antiquity, Greece and Rome. They had their able and resolute women, wives and mothers of princes, who exercised a vast influence —too often a pernicious influence—on the fortunes of their country; but neither in Greece nor in Rome—at least in their palmy days—was there one of whom it could be truly said that she was a mother of her people, not one who beat back the enemies of her country and gave the land rest. Greek and Roman history can produce more than one parallel to Athaliah or to Jezebel, but none to Deborah.

Standing out in Jewish history a unique and stately figure, Deborah is herself a prophecy and a foreshadowing of that larger dispensation, when the Oriental and the Greek ideal of woman—as then most truly fulfilling her mission when seldomest seen and heard—should be cast away as a forgotten thing; when 'in Jesus Christ' there should be 'neither male nor female;' but the sister and the wife, emancipated from their thraldom, should take their place side by side with the brother and the husband, as their counsellors and their friends.

Not indeed that under the Gospel dispensation the prophetess or the judge or the warrior-chieftain should become the normal type of the functions of womanhood, the ideal of the woman's aspirations. For the most part, the Israel of which she is mother will be her own home, her own social circle, her own parish and neighbourhood. By her stronger affections and her finer sensibilities, by her greater sympathy and her truer tact, by her comparative physical weakness, by the direct demands made upon her as a wife and mother, she will commonly be guided to a less conspicuous, but not less useful, sphere of action. The Marys of the Gospel, the Lydia and the Priscilla, the Lois and the Eunice of the apostolic history, these and such as these are the types of Christian womanhood. But ever and again a great crisis will arise, and some heaven-sent heroine will respond to the call. Then it is that the peasant girl will save the most renowned throne in Europe, and the dyer's daughter will restore the most venerated see of

Christendom to its ancient home and its long-lost prestige. But a Joan of Arc and a Catherine of Siena will only appear at long intervals on the stage of this world's history.

A prophecy, but only a prophecy, of the womanhood of the higher dispensation; a shadow of the good things to come, but not the very image. The song of Deborah with all its lofty patriotism, and its exultant faith, is not the utterance of Christian lips. Prophetess though she was, she falls short of the Gospel ideal. Her spirit, as Coleridge[42] finely puts it, is 'the yet not tamed chaos of the spiritual creation.' In 'the fierce and the inordinate' of her utterances, we are 'made to know' through the contrast and 'be grateful for the clearer and the purer radiance which shines on a Christian's path.'

You will have anticipated my reasons for choosing this theme. One subject forces itself on our notice to-day. Met together on the morrow of the festival consecrated to the memory of S. Hilda[43], standing on the ground which she herself trod, and almost beneath the shadow of an ancient sanctuary dedicated in her name, how can we do otherwise than lift up our hearts in thanksgiving to God for her work and example to-day? While our lips have hitherto named only the judge of Israel, the prophetess of Mount Ephraim, our thoughts have reverted to the royal lady, the saintly abbess of Hartlepool and Whitby. How can it be otherwise? The church which we consecrate to-day is the latest fruit of a mighty tree planted by her between twelve and thirteen centuries ago.

It is no strained parallel to compare her with the Hebrew heroine. The period of the Heptarchy was to England what the period of the Judges was to Israel. It was an epoch of ferment and disturbance, a great seething time, when the elements destined to compose the mighty England of the generations to come were still struggling one with another, till at length they settled down, and order was evolved out of chaos. Pagan and believer lived side by side, and fought one with another. Among Christian princes themselves the conflicts were frequent and deadly. Only now and then one king towered above his peers, and forced them to acknowledge his supremacy; just as ever and again one judge in Israel mightier than the rest had been recognised by all the tribes as their supreme ruler. The Church of Christ, having a principle of unity in herself, was the great moral power which composed and harmonized these discordant elements. The unity of the State arose out of the unity of the Church. In this great work of pacification our Northumbrian Deborah bore a conspicuous part. Northumbria was then the centre and focus of light to England. Hilda was in God's hands a chief maker of England, as Deborah was a chief maker of Israel.

But the comparison involves a sharp contrast. Our northern Deborah was a Christian Deborah; like the Hebrew heroine of old, she too led the Lord's hosts against the foe; but unlike her Israelite prototype, the weapons of her warfare were not carnal. There was nothing in her of the fierce untamed spirit, which bristles through the magnificent faith and ardour of the 'great dame of Lapidoth.' Her antagonism was love. Her warfare was peacefulness. By instruction, by example, by discipline, by deeds of kindliness and mercy, she subdued the enemy. We are expressly told that, while in the houses under her care, she studiously inculcated all other virtues such as justice, piety and chastity, yet she laid the chief stress on peace and love. In that last late autumn night, as it were yesterday, ere her spirit departed at cock-crow, she gathered about her her spiritual daughters, and with her waning breath exhorted them to keep peace —the peace of the Gospel—one towards another and towards all men. Though the child of a race of warriors, and herself bearing the name of a Saxon war-goddess", yet she was before all things a woman of peace. Princess and prophetess both, she had her pagan counterparts in the British warrior-queen Boadicea, and the Teutonic seer Veleda. The commanding spirit, the fiery energy, the sense of a divine indwelling, she shared with one or other of them; but the fierceness was subdued, and the exaltation was sanctified, by the transforming power of the word of Christ. The gospel of peace had triumphed. The flame, which a few years earlier had been lighted in Northumbria by the Roman missionary Paulinus, had flickered and died out. The true evangelisation of this northern kingdom commenced with the mission from Iona. Three figures stand out conspicuously in this first planting of the Northumbrian Church. Two of these were Oswald the king, and Aidan the missionary bishop. The third is Hilda, the chief educator of the Northumbrian Church in this its earliest stage— the inaugurator of the work which was afterwards taken up by Benedict Biscop and Bede.

Hilda is closely connected with our own Durham. Of the Northumbrian royal race by birth, she returned at Aidan's bidding to Northumbria for the great work of her life. The Tyne, the Wear, the Hartlepools— these are our three chief centres of population and commerce, and with all these her name is connected. The largest town on the Durham side of the Tyne[45] was originally called after an ancient chapel bearing her name, coeval (it is thought) with the venerable monastery of Jarrow itself—though its later and now common designation is taken from the fisherman's 'sheelings' or sheds. As recently as two centuries ago—after the Restoration—I still find this town described as 'S. Hild's, commonly called Sheelds.' On the northern banks of the Wear again we are told she had a piece of ground allotted to her, and there she established on a small scale her first religious community. But it was in your own Hartlepool that she first became famous. Here she presided for many years over a great religious house, till she migrated hence to the still more famous abbey of Whitby, of which she herself was foundress—the Beacon Bay, as it then was called by a doubly appropriate name, for it became the great centre of spiritual and intellectual light, amidst the darkness of the heathen night, and the twilight of the Christian dawn, to the storm-tossed and shipwrecked on the ocean of ignorance and sin, not in Northumbria only, but throughout the whole of England.

Of this great benefactress of English Christendom unhappily we know but little. All our trustworthy information is contained in two or three pages of Bede. Yet even these scanty notices suggest the features of a striking personality. Of such advantages, social and intellectual, as the age afforded, she seems to have had her full share. She was the daughter of a kingly race, but her stock of experience was enriched by close intercourse with the ignorant and poor. Her spiritual education again was not less wide in its range. Two distinct streams met together in the evangelisation of England. The one was the Roman mission under Augustine, having its head-quarters in Kent; the other was the Celtic mission which issued from S. Columba's Monastery of Iona under Aidan, and settled in our own Northumbria. Both these streams met in Hilda, though her closest associations and her deepest sympathies were with the latter. She had been instructed and baptized in her girlhood, with her kinsfolk, by the Roman missionary Paulinus; and in her mature age she had for her chief adviser and friend the Celtic missionary, Aidan.

Those who live altogether in the world, and those who live altogether apart from the world, both alike miss some valuable elements in the discipline and formation of the character. Neither advantage was denied S. Hilda. Her life, sixty-six years in all, was equally divided. The first half was spent among her kindred in society: during the second half she was an inmate of a religious house.

Her own natural gifts and capacities too, so far as the scanty notices enable us to judge, seem to have fitted her to make good use of these external advantages. To the Celtic and Roman influences of her Christian education she contributed the sterling sober qualities of a Teutonic descent. With the tact and sympathy of a woman, she united the sound judgment and the self-restraint of a man. 'The spirit of wisdom and understanding, the spirit of counsel and ghostly strength' were hers. The great and the lowly alike were drawn towards her. Kings and princes sought her advice in the perplexities of statesmanship; bishops exchanged spiritual counsels with her. Her intellectual sympathies, we may gather, were not less wide than her spiritual, so far as the meagre opportunities of the age gave them scope. Monasteries were then the sole depositories of knowledge, and the sole schools of learning. The religious house with which she was connected was twofold. There was a side for women and a side for men—an arrangement not uncommon in those ages. The chivalry of their Christianity and their race gave the precedence to women. Hilda ruled over both. Her house was a great training school for the clergy. Not less than five of her pupils[46] became bishops of important sees—two of York, one of Dorchester, one of Worcester, and one of Hexham. This last was the famous S. John of Beverley. What wonder that all who came near her saluted her with the endearing name of 'Mother'? a title not as yet, it would seem, given by virtue of their office to abbesses of religious houses, but specially accorded to her, as we are told, by reason of her signal piety and grace. She was indeed a 'Mother in Israel.'

Nor is it only as a school of theology, a nursery of clergy, that her house demands our respect. Here English literature was cradled. The earliest of English poets, Caedmon, the forerunner of Chaucer and of Shakespeare, of Spenser and of Milton, of Wordsworth and Tennyson and Browning, received under Hilda the training and the inspiration which transformed him, like Amos of old, from a simple cowherd into a prophet and teacher of men. If English poetry, in its power, its variety, its richness, surpasses the poetry of any other nation of the modern, perhaps even of the ancient, world, if it be one of God's most magnificent literary gifts to mankind, then we must contemplate with something like reverential awe the house where it was nursed in its infancy.

Did I exaggerate when I classed Hilda among the chief makers of England in the childhood of the English nation? Do not the facts which I have mentioned justify the estimate? Nay, her position was dimly apprehended, even by those who lived near her own time. The story is told by Bede[47], how shortly before her birth her mother dreamt that she found unexpectedly a brilliant necklace in her bosom of such dazzling glory that its lustre penetrated to all parts of Britain. The dream was not a dream.

But Hilda does not stand alone. She was a type, albeit the highest type, of a numerous band of women, more especially in early times, queens and princesses, who realised the prophetic foreshadowing, and became nursing mothers of their own Israel. Shall we forget that the two ancient universities of this land both trace back their spiritual descent to women of royal blood—Oxford to S. Frideswide, and Cambridge to S. Ethelreda? And may we not here note the coincidence that the reigns of three female sovereigns, Elizabeth, Anne, Victoria, mark the three most signal epochs in the history of English literature?

We do well to step aside from time to time from the interests of the present, and record our grateful remembrances of bygone saints and worthies. The oblivion of the past is not a sign of enlightenment. It is rather a token of self-conceit, and self-conceit is blindness. In vain we flatter ourselves that we are giants, because we have a wider range of view than our fathers. We are but the dwarf seated on the giant's shoulders. The progress of mankind is built up on the achievements of successive generations.

But at no time is this lesson more opportune than now. We are met to-day for the consecration of a building which we intend for the chief sanctuary and home of the spiritual work in this district. How can we duly express our thanksgiving for the past? Clergy and laity have worked energetically together. No difference of opinion has disturbed the harmony of action. Liberal gifts have flowed in from all sides. The fabric has been raised far sooner than our highest hopes had foreshadowed. In structure and completeness it surpasses the standard which we had held before our eyes when we commenced. This day's work is the crown of your joy. But, though the crown of your joy, it is only the beginning of your responsibility. The visible edifice is only the scaffolding of the invisible. The energy hitherto directed to the erection of the material fabric must now be concentrated on the spiritual—the building piled up of the souls of men and cemented by faith and love, the temple not made by hands, the sanctuary eternal in the heavens. This henceforward will be the task of you all alike. But meanwhile what form shall our congratulations take? To whom shall the praise be given? Not unto us, O Lord, but rather unto those heroic spirits of the past, the fathers and mothers in Israel who have sown that we might reap; rather unto those silent and faithful workers in successive ages, unknown and unrecorded, who have laboured patiently that we might enter into their labours:

rather unto these, and yet not even unto these, except in a lower degree. 'Not unto us,' nor yet unto them, 'O Lord, but unto Thy name give the praise.' 'The Lord hath been mindful of us, and He shall bless us. He shall bless the house of Israel.'

S. CUTHBERT.

Preached at the Millenary Festival of the
Parish Church of Chester-le-Street.

July 18, 1883.

A thousand years in thy sight are but as yesterday.
PSALM xc. 4.

A THOUSAND years! What a crowd of associations are suggested by these words. What thronging memories of the past, what solemn reflexions on the present, what anxious hopes and fears for the future. A thousand years! What changes have taken place in this long lapse of time. How many nations have risen and fallen; how many dynasties have flourished and decayed; how many tongues have died out; how many once famous names have been forgotten.

A thousand years ago! We cannot by any effort of our imagination realise the condition of England at this remote period. Without a literature, without a parliament, without any of those developments, social, political, and intellectual, which make her what she is. A thousand years ago! When the pirate ancestors of the Conqueror had not yet left their Scandinavian home to settle on the shores of France, and the invasion of England by Norman William was still an event of the remote and unforeseen future. A thousand years ago! When the half-legendary hero of our childhood, the great and wise Alfred, poet, scholar, warrior, legislator, was ruling as king over this land—the one man who deserves to be regarded as the founder of our English literature, the unifier of our English territory, the chief author of our English greatness.

Is it not a striking thought that the opening of the millennium, which we this day commemorate, should have synchronized with the reign of a sovereign who more than any other in the long roll of our history combined in himself, in the fullest measure and in perfect harmony, all those features which are truest and best in the English character? Yes, as we give thanks to God this day for His manifold goodness to ourselves, to this parish, to the Church of this land, let us not forget to mingle with these our thanksgivings the gratitude due to His signal mercy, who in the hour of England's sorest need, when the land was invaded by foreign foes, and darkness—spiritual, intellectual, and social—was gathering fast and thick upon it, raised up this great deliverer, as great as he was wise, as pious and devout as he was great, the noblest type of Englishman who has ever trod this soil. Who can say what would have become of England if Alfred had never been?

A thousand years to man is everything, and more than everything—far transcending the reach of his aims, eluding even the grasp of his imagination. It is, we might almost say, a representation of eternity to him. But to God it is nothing at all. A single day from sunrise to sunset, a night watch come and gone instantaneously for the unconscious slumberer, a fleeting cloud, an arrow's flight, a twinkling of an eye—these images are powerless to describe the nothingness of all measures of time to Him for whom is no before or after, before whose eyes the infinite past and the infinite future are spread as a map, to whom there is one eternal Now.

This contrast, which engages the Psalmist's thoughts in the text, will be impressed upon our minds by the festival of to-day, the contrast between the infinite and the finite, between the eternal mind, the abiding purpose of God, and the fleeting aims, the varying moods, the ever-changing fortunes and vicissitudes of man. For to-day we stand face to face both with the transitory and with the abiding. With the transitory; for as we review this thousand years of history we are reminded how all things human come and go like the shadow of a dream. With the abiding; because through all these changes of civil, of intellectual, of social life, one constant thread of a Divine purpose runs. One institution has survived the wrecks of ages. The Church of Christ is older than the English monarchy, than the English nation, than English law or English literature. The Church of Christ is the same in its essential character now as ever, will be the same to the end of time. It is subject to vicissitudes many and various; it has its triumphs and its defeats; it has its seasons of error and sloth and incapacity and degradation, as well as its seasons of high enterprise and deep spirituality and energetic zeal; for it is administered by human agents. But throughout there has been a sustaining power not of earth; a life-germ which no antagonism of foe, and no recklessness of friend, could extinguish—ever reviving, ever asserting itself, ever breaking out in fresh developments. This power is called in Holy Scripture 'the Word of God.' 'The voice said, Cry; and he said, What shall I cry? All flesh is grass, and all the goodliness thereof is as the flower of the field. The grass withereth; the flower fadeth; but the Word of our God shall stand for ever[48].'

We recall the story of the Book of the Gospels[49], Cuthbert's own book, which the monks of Lindisfarne carried with them in those wanderings that led them at length to the very spot where this day we worship. They set sail for Ireland; a storm arose;

the book fell overboard and was lost; they were driven back to the English coast; disconsolate they went in quest of the precious volume; for a long time they searched in vain; but at length (so says the story) a miraculous revelation was vouchsafed to them, and following its directions they found the book on the sands, far above high-water mark, uninjured by the waves—nay, even more beautiful for the disaster.

Does not this story well symbolize the power of the Eternal Gospel working in the Church? Through the carelessness of man it may disappear amidst the confusion of the storms; the waves may close over it and hide it from human sight. But lost—lost for ever—it cannot be. It must re-assert itself, and its glory will be the greater for the temporary eclipse which it has undergone. Yes, the fate of this Lindisfarne volume of the Gospels is a true type of the undying Word of God, of which it is the written expression.

We celebrate to-day the millenary festival of the foundation of this church. But we must go two centuries farther back still, if we would trace its history to the true source. We place ourselves in imagination twelve centuries ago. We are in a lonely, barren, storm-lashed island off the Northumbrian coast. Cuthbert, the saintly ascetic, has retired thither to his solitary cell—retired, as the event proved, to die. He is there alone with the sea-birds, his cherished companions. For five days the storm prevents all communication with him. Then he is visited by a small company of his monks from Lindisfarne. The end is now at hand. Herefrid, the abbot, is admitted alone. He receives the last instructions of the saint. It is somewhere about midnight, the hour of prayer. The departing saint is strengthened for his long journey with the Communion of the body and blood of Christ. Then raising his hands to heaven 'he sped forth his spirit'—these are Herefrid's own words—' into the joys of the heavenly kingdom.' Herefrid announced his departure to the brethren outside. They were singing the psalm which has justly taken such a prominent place in our service to-day—the psalm, as it so happened, which was appointed in due order for the service of that night, *Deus, repulisti nos*, 'O God, Thou hast cast us out and scattered us abroad, O turn Thee unto us again: O be Thou our help in trouble; for vain is the help of man.' One of the monks mounted the high ground above the cell and held up two lighted torches—one in either hand—the preconcerted signal; and the brothers in far-off Lindisfarne knew that their spiritual father was gone. They too at this very time were chanting the same psalm, *Deus, repulisti nos.* Thus the wail of the Israelites of old was flung across this lonely sea to and fro from island to island—the unpremeditated but fit funeral dirge for him whose destiny in death was stranger than his destiny in life.

The story is recorded by Bede[50], who heard it from Herefrid himself. Herefrid added that the prophetic import of these words was fulfilled shortly after, when several monks were driven forth from Lindisfarne by some perils which assailed them, but God soon built up His Jerusalem again, and restored their scattered remnants. Yet neither Herefrid nor Bede could have foreseen the far stranger fulfilment which was in store long after they were laid in their graves. We may well imagine that the monks of Lindisfarne, as centuries later they wandered to and fro—from north to south, and from sea to sea—bearing the body of S. Cuthbert, knowing not from night to night where they might lay their heads, recalled again and again the Psalmist's wail which had wafted the saint's spirit to the skies, *Deus, repulisti nos*; and when at length they settled in your Chester-le-Street[61], they would remember Bede's narrative, and, again in the words of the Psalmist, break out into thanksgiving, 'The Lord doth build up Jerusalem, and gather together the outcasts of Israel.'

I have spoken of a thousand years, and again of

twelve hundred years; and I have asked you to throw yourselves back in imagination through these long periods, that you may trace the train of events which, in God's providence, has led to the festival of to-day.

But why should you stop here? God's purposes in the chain of cause and consequence are not limited to ten or twelve centuries. I am reminded by the very name of this parish that long before Aidan preached, or Cuthbert was born, God in His far-reaching providence was laying the foundations on which the future Church of Christ in this place should be built. Christ came in the fulness of time—came when all things were prepared for His coming. Not the least important instruments in this preparation were the Romans. Is it not a significant fact that the Evangelist commences his narrative of Christ's human birth and life with the mention of Cæsar Augustus? If we were required to state briefly the services rendered by the Romans as preparing the way for the Gospel, we should say that they were twofold, order and intercommunication. The Romans reduced the nations to order; they consolidated the civilised world; they united it under one rule; they gave it a settled government; they placed it under the administration of justice; they enforced obedience to the laws. This discipline of the world they exercised as a great military power. Again, they provided means of communication between provinces far and wide; they were the greatest road-makers that mankind has ever seen; thus they opened out the known world to travellers. What inestimable benefits these two results of Roman civilisation were to the Apostles and first preachers of the Gospel I need not say. But these very functions are embodied in the name of this place. Chester, *Castra*, the military camp, with its regularity and its discipline, represents the one characteristic, the principle of order. The second part of the name, the *Street*, the Roman road which ran through this place, embodies the other, the benefit of intercommunication. So, then, in the name of your parish, you have a speaking lesson of God's far-seeing designs; and it will give fulness to your thanksgiving to-day if you remember, not only what God has done for you since Christianity was first preached in these parts, but also how, long centuries before, the soil was prepared to receive the seed from the hand of the Divine husbandman.

From the thronging historic memories which this festival more directly recalls, we may single out two great lessons—the influence of a great personality and the discipline of a great public disaster.

1. What was it that won for Cuthbert the ascendancy and fame which no Churchman north of the Humber has surpassed or even rivalled? He

was not a great writer like Bede. He was not a first preacher like Aidan. He founded no famous institution; he erected no magnificent building. He was not martyred for his faith or for his Church. His episcopate was exceptionally short, and undistinguished by any event of signal importance. Whence then this transcendent position which he long occupied, and still to a certain extent maintains?

He owed something doubtless to what men call accident. He was on the winning side in the controversy between the Roman and English observances of Easter. Moreover, the strange vicissitudes which attended his dead body, served to emphasize the man in a remarkable way.

But these are only buttresses of a great reputation. The foundation of the reverence entertained for Cuthbert must be sought elsewhere. Shall we not say that the secret of his influence was this? The 'I' and the 'not I' of S. Paul's great antithesis were strongly marked in him. There was an earnest, deeply sympathetic nature in the man himself, and this strong personality was purified, was heightened, was sanctified by the communion with, the indwelling of, Christ. His deeply sympathetic spirit breathes through all the notices of him. It was this which attracted men to him; it was this which unlocked men's hearts to him. We are told that he had a wonderful power of adapting his instructions to the special needs of the persons addressed. 'He always knew what to say, to whom, when, and how to say it.'

This faculty of reading men's hearts sympathy alone can give. And Cuthbert's sympathy overflowed even to dumb animals. The sea fowl, which bear his name[52], were his special favourites. There is a pleasant story told likewise[53], how on one occasion, being hungry and having no food at hand, he descried an eagle and bade his companion follow it. The attendant returned with a large fish which the eagle had caught in a river. He rebuked his companion, bade him cut the fish in two, and take half back, that God's kindly messenger, the eagle, might not be without a dinner. Other tales too are told—perhaps not altogether legendary—which testify to his sympathy with, and his power over, the lower creation. We are reminded by these traits of other saintly persons of deeply sympathetic nature, of Hugh of Lincoln followed by his tame swan, of Anselm protecting the leveret, of Francis of Assisi conversing familiarly with the fowls of the air and the beasts of the field as with brothers and sisters.

But if the 'I' was thus strong and deep, the 'not I' was not less marked—'Not I, but Christ liveth in me.' His fervour at the celebration of the Holy Sacrament manifested itself even to tears. 'He imitated,' says Bede[4], 'the Lord's Passion which he commemorated, by offering himself a sacrifice to God in contrition of heart.' He died with Christ, that he might live with Christ. We may see many faults in this saint—faults more of the age than of the man. Our reverence for him does not require us to approve the religious ideal which drove him to many years of solitary seclusion, or the religious temper which branded as the worst of heretics those who observed Easter as their forefathers had observed it. But these errors may well be condoned in one, of whom it can be truly said that 'his life was hidden with Christ in God.' As we read Bede's life of him, amidst much credulous superstition we are struck with the entire absence of that taint of Mariolatry which poisoned the well-springs of a later theology. God in Christ, Christ in God—this is all in all to him.

2. But let me turn for a few moments to the other great lesson which the memories of to-day suggest,—the discipline of a period of disaster. The Israelite sojourn in the desert—the wanderings to and fro, the privations, the trials, the defeats—this is the prototype of many a chapter in the history of churches, when God has led His people into the wilderness—not to crush them, not to annihilate them, but in the prophet's words, 'to speak comfortably' to them, to chastise with a fatherly chastisement,

to amend, to purify, to strengthen, to train for a greater future. So it was with these Lindisfarne monks. We may smile at their credulity. We may contemn their ignorance. We may scout their old-world superstitions. But for those who have eyes to see and ears to hear, there is a sublimity of heroism in the faith, the constancy, the unfailing courage of these outcast wanderers, carrying about the body of their spiritual ancestor, 'perplexed but not in despair, persecuted but not forsaken, cast down but not destroyed,' reaching at length their goal and finding in Durham a greater Lindisfarne—a sublimity of Christian heroism which no superficial errors can hide.

We meet together to-day with no common feelings of joy and gratitude. We pour out our hearts in thanksgiving to God for His manifold and great mercies to the Church in this place during the thousand years past. We beseech Him to accept this fabric, renovated and adorned, as a feeble offering of His grateful servants. We supplicate Him to look favourably upon us in the years to come. The future is hidden from our eyes. We know not—we cannot know—what the next millennium, the next century, even the next decade, will bring forth. We look forward with the brightest hopes indeed, but not without many grave anxieties also. It may be that in some form or other He will try us again, will lead us once more into the wilderness, will renew once more the discipline of the Lindisfarne wanderers. If such a trial should await us, then may we, with our higher enlightenment and our larger knowledge, not fall short of their patience and courage and hope. May our faith find expression once more in the old familiar words of the Psalmist, full of power and of pathos, which in successive generations have touched and solaced the hearts of mourners over the open grave: 'Lord, Thou hast been our refuge from one generation to another,' ' Thou art God from everlasting and world without end;' 'A thousand years in Thy sight are but as yesterday;' 'When Thou art angry, all our days are gone;' 'Turn Thee again, O Lord, at the last; and be gracious unto Thy servants,' *'Deus, repulisti,' 'Domine, refugium.'*

THE DEATH OF BEDE.

Preached at the Consecration of S. Peter's Church, Jarrow.

S. Peter's Day, 1881.

It is finished.

S. JOHN xix. 30.

Do you ask why I have chosen these particular words for my text? I will answer the question by telling you a story. It is an old story, well-known everywhere, but best known here (at least I should suppose) in this town of Jarrow where I am speaking; a story well-worn, but not worn out, old but fresh still, fresh with the freshness of perpetual youth.

A man past the middle of life lay on his death-bed, surrounded by his disciples. They were sorrowing, says a bystander who relates the incident[55], at the thought that they should see his face no more in this life. A youth was taking down some words from the master's lips. 'One chapter still remains,' said the lad, 'of the book which thou hast dictated; and yet it seems troublesome to thee to ask more of thee.' 'It is not troublesome,' said the dying man, 'get out thy pen and prepare, and write quickly.' So the hours went on. At intervals he conversed with his scholars; then again he dictated. At length his amanuensis turned to him; 'Beloved master, one sentence only remains to be written.' 'Good,' he replied, 'write it.' After a short pause the boy told him that it was written. 'Good,' said he, 'it is finished; thou hast said truly.' And in a few moments more he gave up his soul to God, with his last breath chanting the doxology, familiar to him, as to us.

You have recognised the story[56]. The dying man was Bede; the book, which he dictated, was the translation of S. John's Gospel into the English tongue.

So then these solemn words 'It is finished,' appropriate at all times and in all places, have a singular propriety in this place and at this time; in this place which (whatever other and varied interests it may have for you) is known to the world at large chiefly as the home of Bede the Venerable; at this time, when the recent appearance[57] of the latest English translation of the Scriptures may well recall our minds to the earliest.

'It is finished.' These words were full of meaning to the dying man. Three completions, three endings, more especially they appear to have suggested to his mind.

1. There was first of all the finishing of the work of dictation, on which he was engaged. When his

youthful amanuensis used the words (as he appears to have done), it probably did not occur to him that they were the very words of the dying Saviour on the Cross. The last chapter, the last sentence, was written. The loving labour, on which they had been so long engaged, was ended. His dear master had lived to see the completion. It was with much joy, which even the sad thought of the approaching severance could not quench, that he announced, 'It is finished.'

The incident was indeed memorable, far more memorable than it could have appeared to any there present, to the translator, to the amanuensis, to the sorrowing circle of scholars who stood around awaiting the departure of their dear master. It was satisfaction enough for them to think that one Gospel—the chief Gospel—was now clothed in a language which the people could understand. They could not foresee the long, glorious, and eventful history of the English Bible, of which this was the opening scene. To ourselves its true significance will appear. The names of Wicliffe and Tyndale, of Rogers and Coverdale, of a long line of martyrs and confessors in the cause of Biblical knowledge and truth, will rise up before us. To ourselves it will recall the time, the thought, the labour, expended upon this work of translation in later generations, when it passed from individuals, who took it upon themselves of their own zeal and love, to committees and bodies of men duly authorised to exercise a common judgment. To ourselves it will seem to link the far-off past with the immediate present, the age of Bede with the age of the Victorian revisers.

What is the meaning of all this? What significance is there in the fact, that age after age so much thought and labour has been expended over this one book? Whatever else may come of this latest revision, one result at least has been achieved. It is a striking testimony to the power, the worth, the pricelessness of the book itself. Why is it that fifty or sixty men have been content—yes, and more than content—to spend years upon the work, to take long journeys from the most distant parts of the kingdom, to give their time and their thoughts gratuitously, without even the hope of fame,—for the achievement is the achievement of a committee, and the individual reaps no glory? Without the hope of fame, did I say? Nay, with the absolute certainty of censure, of rebuke, of misinterpretation, of imputation of motives, of adverse criticism of all kinds. Did their predecessors—better men than they—their predecessors, whether individuals or committees, receive any better treatment? Was not our present Authorised Version, which all men now with justice esteem so highly, decried on its first appearance, accused of faults which it had, and faults which it had not, of bad English, of bad scholarship, of bad theology? Did not almost every one say then, as almost everyone says now, 'The old is better?' Nay, if the recent revisers are surprised at all by the public criticisms on their work, it is by their mildness, not by their harshness. Judging from the experience of the past, they looked for a far more severe verdict on their work than has been pronounced. Why then did they undertake this thankless task with their eyes open? Why, except that there is a power, a life, a spell, in that book which drew them by its magic? They held it an honour, a privilege, as well as an obligation, to do what they could to set that book before the English-speaking people in the best form which improved scholarship and enlarged knowledge suggested. And now, with a feeling akin to that which suggested the words to Bede's young amanuensis eleven or twelve centuries ago, they say thankfully, 'It is finished.'

2. But the words, as they were taken up and repeated by Bede, had a second meaning also. 'It is finished,' said the youth. 'Good,' replied Bede, 'it is finished. Thou hast said truly.' The lad spoke of the volume of parchment, of the writing in ink. But there was another writing written to the end, another volume closed, at that same hour, the writing of an earthly

career, the volume of a human life—holy, brave, zealous, patient, scholarly, loving—for which Englishmen, and not Englishmen only, are bound to thank and to praise the great Head of the Church to all time. All the struggles of an intense and feeling heart were stilled; all the efforts of an assiduous and eager intellect were lulled to rest; all the conflicts of a sensitive and anxious conscience were hushed in peace. The last letter was spelt out; the last line was penned; the volume was closed, the first volume, the volume of Time. The next volume would open in Eternity. It was a solemn moment for him. It was a solemn moment for us, for all English Christians, but for you men and women of Jarrow more especially, who are the trustees of his good deeds, and the heirs of his fame.

3. I have traced two meanings of these words 'It is finished,' as they were spoken during this last scene of Bede's life. But is it possible to stop here? Can we fail to see a reference to them, as they were spoken seven centuries before by Him who spake as never man spake, spoken not at the supreme moment of an individual life, not when the volume of a saintly career was closed, but spoken in the supreme moment of the Life of Lives, spoken over the closing of a volume in human history? When Bede repeats with such marked emphasis the words *Consummatum est*,

'It is finished,' is it not clear that he was carried away in imagination from the scenes immediately surrounding him, saw the Saviour's body hanging on the Cross of Calvary, and heard from His dying lips those last words announcing the completion of man's redemption, words which not long before he must have dictated to his youthful scribe? What without the hopes inspired by these words were his literary works? What was his laborious life? Mere beating of the air, nothing more. What without this hope was his approaching death? Blank despair, nothing less. Yes, all was completed in that sacrifice. The prophecies were fulfilled; the types were realised; the shadows were replaced by the substance. Sin was vanquished. Death was annihilated. The full ransom was paid, the full ransom for the sins of mankind, for the sins of him Bede, for the sins of you and me. All was over. Old things had passed away. All things had become new. The volume was closed.

This hope, this joy, this glory, shone over the death-bed of Bede. God grant that, when our time comes, it may in like manner irradiate ours, yours and mine.

But a great completion is after all only a great commencement. Wherever we say 'It is finished,' we say in effect 'It is beginning.' The goal of the past is the starting point of the future. 'Except a corn of wheat fall into the ground and die, it abideth alone; but if it die, it bringeth forth much fruit.' 'Except it die' is written across the face of the spiritual world, not less than across the face of the natural. Dissolution, decay, disappearance, death, this is the condition of life. Through death all things pass into life. Is it not so in all the three cases, to which the words 'It is finished' are applied in Bede's dying words?

We say 'It is finished' of a book. To its author it is dead. But then only its true life begins. Like the corn of wheat, it is sown in the ground. If it is a fertile book, it springs up, and blossoms, and bears fruit a hundred or a thousand fold. Generations come and go, but still it blossoms, still it fructifies. I referred before to the Revised Translation of the New Testament. We have witnessed here a phenomenon altogether without a parallel in the history of literature. The demand for it has far outstripped any past experience of publishers, has far surpassed the sanguine expectations of the most sanguine. It is sold at every railway stall and canvassed in every newspaper. And yet this is not a novel, not a sensational story, not a book of travel or adventure; but an old trite well-worn book, on which some time and patience has been bestowed to make it speak more clearly to English readers. What the future of this Revision may be, we know not. This is in God's hands. But, if nothing else should come from it, was it not worth all the time and all the labour thus to stimulate, as it has stimulated, the reading of God's Holy Word, thus to arrest the attention of the careless and indifferent, thus to gather crowds about the book of books, as more than three centuries ago they were gathered at the first appearance of the English Bible round the reader[58], reading from the copy chained to the desk in our great churches and cathedrals? May we not hope that some consciences will be pricked, some hearts will be stirred, some souls will be won to Christ? May we not cherish the belief that not a few who came to criticise will remain to pray?

But if 'It is finished' means 'It is now beginning' in the case of a book, it means this equally in the case of a good man. Of him it is true, most true, that, though dead, he liveth. Nay, we may go further and say that, *because* dead, he liveth. The good work which he did, the good cause which he advocated, the good example which he left, these remain, these blossom and bear fruit. Their growth, their fertility is no longer impeded by any feuds and jealousies in others, by any imperfections—faults of temper, or of judgment, or of tact—in the man himself. At length they have free course. More than eleven centuries have rolled away since Bede trod the soil of Jarrow. And still his name is fresh among you. Still his work, his influence, his example, are potent for good. Still, as far and wide, in the busy upstart towns of the Transatlantic West, and in the quiet immemorial cities of ancient India, men read the simple story of his dying hours, the aspiration rises in their hearts, 'Let me die the death of the righteous, and let my last end be like his.'

And if this be true of the finishing of a book, of the finishing of a man's career, it is in a far higher and fuller sense true of that great finishing, that ending of all endings, the ending on the Cross. That death was life indeed, the life of the world. That finishing was the great beginning of a heavenly kingdom, the beginning of a rescue of souls from sin and death, the beginning of an ingathering of a holy people of God, the foundation of a second and spiritual temple, the Church of Christ.

The ingathering of a people, the foundation of a temple. As I utter these words I am recalled to the purpose for which we are met together to-day. There is a special sense in which you too—like the boy scribe of Bede, like Bede himself—will repeat the words 'It is finished' to-day. 'It is finished,' the material fabric, the building made with hands, the walls, the pillars, the roof, the furniture. All is complete. Nothing is wanting. A district will shortly be formed. An incumbent has already been named. This parish will enter upon a new and independent career. On this day—S. Peter's Day—we consecrate this building with solemn prayer to Almighty God, as the church of S. Peter. In some branches of the Church of Christ two Apostles are commemorated together on this day. It is the day not of S. Peter only, but of S. Peter and S. Paul. So we here link the two Apostles together. We associate the new church and parish of S. Peter with the old church and parish of S. Paul, that (like the two Apostles of old) they may live and labour and suffer together, as fellow-workers for Christ.

And what will be the predominant feeling of all who take part in this day's work? Must it not be thanksgiving, thanksgiving from a full heart and with joyful lips? Thanksgiving, first and foremost, from those whom God has prompted to build this house, that their heart's desire has been realised, and that they are permitted this day to see this church consecrated to the honour of God and to the edification of His people; thanksgiving from the clergy that now at length they have a fit sanctuary for the worship of Almighty God, where the voice of prayer and praise shall be heard continually, a fit abode where all the pious feelings and all the hallowed memories of the neighbourhood shall find a home in the future; thanksgiving, lastly, from the people at large, that God has dealt so graciously with them, that He has prompted the hearts of His servants, the donors, to this pious work, and that from their hands they, the congregation, receive it without money and without price.

A feeling of thanksgiving first; and what next? A sense, a strong, a growing, an overpowering sense, of responsibility. Ah, yes, here, as elsewhere, 'It is finished,' will mean 'It is only now beginning.' The material temple is built; the fabric made with hands is completed. And now begins that larger, more arduous, more protracted work of building up the spiritual fabric, the sanctuary not made with hands, of piling up and cementing together the souls of men, that the building may rise ever higher and higher, and wax ever stronger and stronger, a glorious edifice, a mighty fortress of truth and righteousness, an holy temple acceptable to the Lord.

Therefore I ask your prayers, your earnest prayers, for the services which shall be held in this church, and the congregations which shall be gathered therein. But above all I beseech you to lift up voice and heart for him who shall be entrusted with the care of this new parish, for him who—neither unknown nor unapproved before—henceforward will enter upon a larger work; that he may stir up the gift of God that is in him; that he may ever have in remembrance into how high a dignity and how weighty an office and charge he is called; that he may make full proof of his ministry; and that thus living and labouring, spending and being spent, he may so fight the good fight, may so finish his course, that he may receive the crown of righteousness, which the Lord, the righteous Judge, shall give him in that day.

'Then cometh the end;' then, and not till then. Then at length all is finished. Then the grave shall give up her dead. Then the seals shall be broken and the books shall be opened. Then we all, you and I, shall stand before the judgment-seat of Christ, stript of our disguises, that we may receive each according to his works. God grant that we may find joy and peace in that terrible, that glorious day.

RICHARD DE BURY.

Preached in Durham Cathedral, at the Jubilee Commemoration of Durham University.

S. Peter's Day, 1882.

Let us now praise famous men and our fathers that begat us.... Their seed shall remain for ever, and their glory shall not be blotted out. Their bodies are buried in peace; but their name liveth for evermore.

ECCLESIASTICUS xliv. 1, 13, 14.

Quid retribuam Domino pro omnibus quae retribuit mihi?—'What shall I render unto the Lord for all the benefits that He hath rendered to me?'

This question is asked in the Psalmist's words by an eminent bishop of Durham[59] more than five centuries ago, the most learned man of his country and age. The answer, as might be expected, is a scholar's answer. He had asked himself again and again, he writes[60], what pious service would best please the Most High God and confer the greatest benefit on the Church Militant; and lo, a troop of poor scholars presented themselves to the eye of his mind.

These were they who might have grown up into strong pillars of the Church; but, though thirsting for knowledge after the first taste, and apt students of the liberal arts, yet for the sake of a livelihood, they were forced, by a sort of apostasy, to return to mechanic pursuits, to the great loss of the Church and to the degradation of the whole clergy. So, he adds, his compassionate affection took the special form of providing poor scholars not only with the exigencies of life but also with a supply of useful books.

Here breathes the noblest spirit of the munificent benefactors in the past. What shall be the spirit of our response, who are the recipients of such benefactions? For this same question, which Richard of Bury asked himself many centuries ago, must be asked and answered to ourselves by us on this our Jubilee Celebration, 'What shall *we* render unto the Lord for all His benefits?'

The words of the text will be familiar to not a few here, as forming part of the special lesson in the Commemoration Service in many of our older collegiate and academic foundations. They will suggest an answer to our question, though only a partial answer. If we can do nothing else, we will at least pour out our hearts in thanksgiving this day; we will praise famous men of old, our ancient benefactors, our spiritual and intellectual forefathers, that through our praises their good deeds may redound to the honour and glory of God.

But how can we appropriate such language to ourselves? Our University is the child of yesterday. It cannot trace its pedigree back through a long line of illustrious ancestry. This day's gathering places the fact beyond the reach of concealment or self-deception. We have among us the first proctor[61], the earliest fellow, one, perhaps more than one, of the original undergraduates of Durham, still active and vigorous with a prospect of some years of usefulness before God shall call them to their account. All this reminds us that we are still young, very young.

Very young, yes; but very old at the same time. It has been the special privilege of this University, that, though so recently created, it inherits traditions and associations, not less ancient and not less sacred than those which cluster about the walls of the most venerable colleges in Oxford or Cambridge. Is it a small thing that you are housed in the Norman keep of the Conqueror and the unique gallery of Pudsey and the lofty and spacious hall of Hatfield and Fox[62], that, together with these relics of a splendid past, there are stamped on your walls the arms of Tonstall, of Cosin, of Crewe, of Butler, of Barrington—of the wise, gentle, loving, learned pastor, of the diligent, precise, æsthetic, loyal, ecclesiastical ruler, of the munificent, open-handed donor, of the profound, reverential, modest Christian philosopher, of the large-hearted, kindly philanthropist and patron of education—thus holding ever before your eyes the memorials of all that is truest and best, all that is most instructive and most inspiring, in the later history of the Durham Episcopate, all those several elements which combined make up the ideal of the Christian scholar and the Christian minister, the man of God made perfect, throughly furnished unto all good works? And again I ask, is it an insignificant privilege that your University has grown up beneath the shelter of this venerable Cathedral, with all its rich historic associations, with all its glories of architectural genius and skill, with that singularly happy combination of human art and natural feature which renders Durham unique among the cathedrals of England—I might almost say, of Christendom? And last of all, as you meet morning after morning amidst the architectural monuments of Pudsey and Langley in the Galilee, do you not reflect with reverence and thanksgiving—you teachers and you students—that, kneeling there in prayer, you have in your midst a far more impressive memorial than these in the simple tomb of a great man[63] of the remoter past, pious, gentle, affectionate, studious, learned—a true pattern for all scholars and all masters to the end of time?

Have you eyes to see? Here then is your historical inheritance; and what fairer estate could you desire? Here is your ancient lineage; and what more illustrious ancestry could any student boast? Yours are the associations which inspire; yours is the nobility which obliges. You are surrounded by a great cloud of witnesses. On you a necessity, a strong necessity, is laid.

1. I bid you bear me company, first of all, while I journey far back into the remote past, and I will show you the cradle of your race. The time is the middle of the sixth century. The scene is a lonely island off the western coast, beaten by the Atlantic surge. This Iona—this bleak, barren patch of land—is the spiritual and intellectual metropolis of Western Christendom. Here is the centre of civilisation, of learning, of light and truth for the nations. Here is the simple home, which dependent seats of study and evangelistic work recognise as their mother. Here lives the simple presbyter to whom bishops and Churches in far distant lands bow as their acknowledged chief and guide. From Columba's monastery Aidan goes forth on his mission to Northumbria. The Holy Island on the eastern coast answers to

the Holy Island on the western. The beacon fire of Lindisfarne flashes on the glorious light signalled from the beacon fire of Iona. Aidan, settled in his new home, gathers about him twelve pupils—true image of the apostolic College. This little band of scholars is the foreshadowing, the forerunner, the true inauguration of your University of Durham. Ah, fellow-students, is it not an inspiring thought for you and for me, that through the long darkness of the ages these streamers of our northern aurora shot their glories glowing and quivering athwart the midnight sky, and gladdened the souls of men?

2. Now again retrace your steps and travel forward through a century. What do you then find? The central light of Christendom is no longer on that lonely western island. It must be sought now between the banks of the Tyne and the Wear. In his twin monasteries Benedict Biscop[64] collects together all the best learning and all the best art of his time. A great traveller himself, he accumulates in these his homes the appliances of civilisation and instruction acquired on his many travels. Whatever lessons Ireland or Gaul or Rome were able to teach are gathered into a focus there. S. Peter at Wearmouth and S. Paul at Jarrow are the two eyes of religion and education. The learning of Benedict Biscop's foundations culminates in Bede. He was diligent beyond the common

diligence of the student. He was versed in all the knowledge accessible in his day. He wrote largely and on divers subjects. He lived writing, and he died writing. And his position too in the transmission of learning through the dark ages was unique. The torch which had been passed from Iona through Lindisfarne to Jarrow was transmitted by Bede's hands from Jarrow to York. Through Alcuin's school at York[65] the light of learning was diffused over Western Christendom, and gleamed through the midnight till the dawn of a brighter day. Again, I say, what a thought is this for you, you worshippers round the tomb of Bede.

3. An interval of several hundred years elapses. We have now reached the middle of the thirteenth century, a marvellous age of precocious literary, artistic, and political activity, in which England held a foremost place—the era of Roger Bacon and Robert Grosseteste and Simon de Montfort—the dawn of scientific invention, the birth-time of our parliamentary institutions, the zenith of scholastic philosophy, an age of architectural genius and fertility to which the history of mankind offers no parallel. It was likewise the age of great academic developments. Then it is that we trace the first beginnings of a collegiate system, which, though not confined to English universities, has in them struck deeper roots,

and attained a fuller and fairer growth, than elsewhere. Of this magnificent tree Durham claims the honour of sowing the seed. The earliest of our existing colleges owes its origin to the munificence of William of Durham[66], the founder of University College, Oxford. His example was rapidly followed by Walter of Merton in Oxford, and Hugh of Balsham in Cambridge. From that time forward colleges grew and multiplied, till they became, as they continue to this day, the pride and glory, the distinctive characteristic, of our old English academic institutions. Thus when a later William of Durham[67], fifty years ago, taking counsel with the Dean and Chapter of his day, resolved with them to found a university here, which should not only be an examining body, like the coeval University of London, should not only maintain a professorial staff for the education of students, like the universities of foreign lands, but should likewise embody in itself, as an integral part of its system, the collegiate life of the older universities, and when for this purpose he resigned the old palace-fortress of his princedom to be the home of such a college, he did but tread in the footsteps of his namesake, the father of the colleges of England. University College, Durham, founded by the liberality of an Oxford man in the nineteenth century, was the just recognition and return for

University College, Oxford, founded by the munificence of a Durham man in the thirteenth.

4. We pass over another century. The character of the age is changed. The hopes of the thirteenth century were not realised by the fourteenth. The promise of a rich harvest had been cruelly blighted. The religious orders had fallen away from their first love, equally in their spiritual aspirations and in their intellectual earnestness. There was a general decay of learning. The age of feudalism was gone; the age of chivalry was waning. Old things were fast passing away; and yet the new order had not taken their place. Troubles within and without were multiplying. There were fierce internal struggles, the forerunners of the still more terrible civil conflicts of the Roses. The brilliant but ruinous continental wars had begun—destined for some generations by their phantom glory to lure England aside from the path of true progress. There was much splendour still, but it was the splendour of the full-blown flower which the first breath of wind scatters in desolation. In this age of growing gloom, the bishop's manor-house at Auckland shone like a bright star in the darkness. Richard of Bury would have been remarkable in any age. He was 'a man,' writes Petrarch[68], 'of fervid genius.' In an age when books were scarce, his rooms were strewn with books. He had gathered

them together from far and near, at home and abroad. They were his cherished companions, his bosom friends. But it is not as the devoted student and the widely-read scholar that he deserves our attention to-day. He was also the patron of academic learning in a novel way. His rich library—rich at least according to the ideas of the time—he left to Oxford. The poor scholars of William of Durham, the nucleus of University College, were not the only Durham foundation at Oxford. There was also a Durham College—developed at a later date into Trinity College—an offshoot and dependency of the Benedictine monastery of this cathedral—endowed and consolidated, if not founded, by this Richard of Bury. And we reflect with pleasure to-day, that this foundation, which traces its origin to Durham, has repaid the debt thus incurred by giving to your University the present heads of your two colleges. But it was another act of reciprocation which I had chiefly in view when I named Durham College in Oxford. To this college Bishop Richard left his rich collection of books for the use of the University at large, giving very minute directions how they should be preserved, and under what cautions they should be lent[69]. This, so far as we know, was the first beginning of a university or college library in England on any considerable scale—the true progenitor of the Bodleian. Thus here again, as in the case of collegiate foundations, the honour of the prerogative act rests with Durham; and when some thirty years ago Martin Routh, the venerable head of Magdalen College, bequeathed his excellent library to you, he only followed the precedent, and reciprocated the benefaction, of a bishop of Durham five centuries earlier.

5. I will ask you again to travel with me two centuries further down the highway of time. The death-warrant of the old order is issued. Not England only, but all Europe, is convulsed with the birth-throes of a new age. The great Reformation has swept away the monastic houses. The cathedral foundations have been reconstituted. Dean and Canons have taken the place of Prior and Monks. So far Durham did not fare differently from any other cathedral. But the academic traditions specially connected with Durham were not forgotten in the general change. The obligations imposed by the connexion with Durham College, Oxford, were recognised; and in the charter it was stated as one main intention of the foundation that youth should be instructed in liberal studies. But beyond the boys of the Grammar School, the idea recognised in the charter found no realisation in fact.

6. Again another century elapses. It is once more a season of upheaval and convulsion. A

8—2

political revolution has taken the place of a religious. At this crisis the project of an academic foundation at Durham is definitely revived. The Lord Protector[10] is petitioned to found a college here. The petition is granted on the ground that it may conduce to 'the promoting of learning and piety in these poor, rude, and ignorant parts'; and so an institution is created, bearing the title of 'the Master or Provost, Fellows and Scholars of the College of Durham, of the foundation of Oliver, Lord Protector of the Commonwealth of England, Scotland, and Ireland.' But the death-stroke of the Protector was the death-stroke of this institution. In the words of a contemporary complaint it was by his decease 'left an orphan, scarce bound up in its swaddling clothes.' The University of Durham was not destined to have such a beginning.

7. Once again there is a lapse of two centuries; and the hope so long deferred is at length fulfilled. The institution which had been foreshadowed amidst the agonies of the great Reformation, which had been prematurely attempted amidst the troubles of the great Revolution, was born into life with the birth-throes of the Reform Bill. The college, which Cromwell had designed to build upon the ruins of the Chapter and the episcopate, was at length founded by the joint action of the bishop and the capitular body. The Palatine jurisdiction had had its day. Its glories

passed away, not without many regrets. But it stood condemned as an anachronism. A more appropriate, though less dazzling, environment was henceforward to encircle the see of S. Cuthbert. The distinctive coronet of the Durham mitre[71] assumed a new meaning. There is a crown of knowledge, as well as a diadem of sovereignty. The last Lord of the Palatinate became the first Visitor of the University. Van Mildert[72] was the fit link of transition between the old and the new —at once the prince of lordly hospitality and munificence, and the scholar of student tastes and feeble health and simple abstemious habits of life. The foundation of the University was a matter of anxious and absorbing care to him. 'The excitement,' he writes, 'occasioned by the intense interest of the subject now constantly occupying my thoughts is more than a broken constitution like mine will bear; and before our projects can have taken root I fear my feeble energies will have withered away; but if the cause thrives, the sacrifice of the remainder of a brief existence here will have been well made.' Touching words these, which should secure for him a large place in your heart, as you had a large place in his.

Of others your founders and benefactors the time would fail me to tell. Of those rulers and instructors —early and late—to whose wise supervision and patient teaching and energetic labours this University is hardly, if at all, less indebted than to its benefactors in a narrower sense, this is not the place to speak. But these will not be forgotten by you, as you lift up your hearts in thanksgiving to God in praise of your spiritual and intellectual fathers, 'by their knowledge of learning meet for the people, wise and eloquent in their instructions[73].' Heirs of the traditions of Iona and Lindisfarne, of Jarrow and Wearmouth! Sons of Columba and Aidan and Bede! Latest born of a long line of illustrious forefathers, remember what is due to this ancestry, what is due to your own generation, what is due to yourselves. Above all and before all, remember what is due to God, the giver of all. *Fundamenta vestra super montibus sanctis*[74]. 'Your foundations are on the holy mountains.' 'Other foundation can no man lay than that which is laid.' Forget not this. Then in the far-off ages to come, as they sing the praises of their fathers which begat them, remote generations will say of you, as you say of those your forerunners and benefactors in the distant past, 'The Lord hath wrought great glory by them through His great power[75].' Then the ruthless storms of circumstance will beat against your house, and the devastating flood of time will sweep over it, in vain; for it is founded upon a rock—the Rock of Zion, the Rock of Ages.

From Richard of Bury I started; with Richard of

Bury let me end. When Bishop Richard's soul migrated hence, his four seals, we are told, were delivered to the Chapter and broken up; and from the precious metal thus obtained was fashioned a chalice[76] for the sanctuary of this Cathedral. These things are an allegory, are they not? All our characteristic gifts, all our inherited privileges, all our official opportunities and powers, all that bears the impress of the man, all that is typified by the seals—what nobler destination for these, than that, melted and fused in the Great Refiner's fire, they should be remoulded into a vessel of the Spirit, meet for the House of God, fulfilled with the graces and benedictions which flow from the crucified Christ, that they may be poured out thence and dispensed for the strength and solace and refreshment of the souls of men?

BERNARD GILPIN.

PREACHED IN THE PARISH CHURCH OF HOUGHTON-LE-SPRING, AT THE TERCENTENARY COMMEMORATION OF BERNARD GILPIN.

Feast of S. Philip and S. James, 1884.

Be ye thankful.

COLOSSIANS iii. 15.

THANKFULNESS—the feeling of the heart—thanksgiving—the expression of that feeling—these hold a foremost place, I had almost said, the foremost place among the duties of Christ's servants in the teaching of S. Paul.

It is so here. Quite unexpectedly, quite abruptly, the injunction is thrust upon his readers. It has no special reference to what has gone before; it is no obvious introduction to what follows after. But it must have a place. Whether in season or out of season, it matters not. This duty of thankfulness, this obligation of thanksgiving, must not be forgotten. It is of all times and all places. Nor is the Apostle satisfied with once enforcing it. Two verses lower down he repeats it with increased emphasis, lest it should be overlooked: 'Whatsoever ye do in word or deed, do all in the name of the Lord Jesus, giving thanks to God and the Father by Him.' It must be the never-failing accompaniment of every word uttered, of every action done.

And so elsewhere. A thanksgiving forms the all but universal commencement of his letters. Thanksgiving is the crown of Christian worship; thanksgiving is the purpose for which the Church exists. The glory, which redounds to God through the thanksgiving of His people, is the ultimate end and aim of their being. The thankful heart, the thankful lips, the thankful life, these alone fulfil the purpose for which they were created.

And the Church has caught up and prolonged the Apostle's teaching. To the highest act of Christian worship, to the service which links us most closely with our Lord, the Holy Communion of His Body and Blood, she has given, as its proper right, the title of thanksgiving, Eucharist; thanksgiving for God's gift of His only-begotten, thanksgiving for the sacrifice upon the Cross, thanksgiving for our participation in that sacrifice, for our cleansing and sanctification through the shedding of that blood. In that one eucharistic service we gather up, as it were, all special thanksgivings for all special mercies, we fulfil the apostolic injunction. 'Do all in the name of the

Lord Jesus, giving thanks to God and the Father by Him.' The transcendent mercy of Christ's death on the Cross, which we set forth in that Holy Sacrament, unites, harmonizes, illumines, glorifies all lesser mercies which we owe to God's goodness.

But while thanksgiving is never misplaced and never ill-timed, it is nowhere more appropriate than on an exceptional occasion like the present, the day of S. Philip and S. James, set apart as the tercentenary commemoration of your own local saint and hero, Bernard Gilpin[77]. Whether we consider the festival of our Church calendar, or whether we contemplate the epoch of which the tercentenary celebration reminds us, or whether our eyes are centred on the particular man, we have abundant cause for thanksgiving.

1. First and foremost; what sources of thankfulness does the apostolic anniversary itself suggest? If the festival of S. Thomas teaches the lesson of doubts overruled, and scepticism convinced, by the power of the Cross; if the festival of S. Matthew presents to us the temptations of secular callings overcome, and worldliness sanctified, by the presence of Christ; if the festival of S. Stephen throws a halo of glory over the sufferer for Christ, and administers strength and comfort to the persecuted, has not the festival of S. Philip and S. James likewise its special message to our souls? What corresponding lessons

of thanksgiving do the notices of Philip, the foremost of these two Apostles, suggest? Our thoughts are recalled to those earliest scenes on the shores of the Galilean lake, the very birthday of the Church of Christ. Philip belongs to the first group of four—all natives of Bethsaida, 'the house of fishing'—who at Christ's calling left their all and followed Him, that they might become fishers of men. But this name not only reminds us of the first foundation of the Church of Christ. It recalls likewise the universality of His Church. Philip summons to Jesus' presence Nathanael, the true Israelite in whom there is no guile. Philip—the same Philip—is afterwards the means of introducing to the Master those Greeks who came to worship at the feast, the first and only Greeks of whom we read in such a connexion. Thus he is the forerunner of a Stephen, the forerunner of a Paul. In his action he typifies the great truth, which the Church embodies, that Christ recognises no distinction between race and race. I seem to see therefore why the framers of our present Lectionary, while they provided special lessons for this festival in the three other cases, permitted the second lesson for the evening service alone to remain undisturbed, as it occurred in the ordinary course of scripture reading—this third chapter of the Epistle to the Colossians,—because in it is enunciated the great principle which was embodied in the few notices of Philip's work; 'There is neither Greek nor Jew, circumcision nor uncircumcision, barbarian, Scythian, bond nor free; but Christ is all, and in all.' Yes, at length the visions of psalmist and prophet are fulfilled; the distant islands bring their offerings to the God of Israel; the children of the far-off North gather together to the sanctuary of the spiritual Jerusalem. So then, when we commemorate Philip's work, we are reminded of all the vast consequences which flowed from his initial act, flowed ceaselessly and are flowing still through the long centuries—of Paul, the great Apostle of the Gentiles; of Columba, our spiritual forefather, the abbot of lonely Iona; of Aidan, the gentle, sympathetic, devoted missionary, the first evangelist of these Northumbrian shores. Should we not therefore open wide the flood-gates of our thanksgiving, that it may flow freely, and rise up to the throne of grace? We, the Gentiles, we, the barbarous islanders of the far-off West, are the direct heirs of Philip's work transmitted through the ages.

2. But secondly; the word 'Tercentenary' suggests another abundant topic of thankfulness.

We are reminded of the great crisis—the greatest in the long course of its history—through which the Church passed three hundred years ago. The life of Bernard Gilpin spanned the whole period of the

English Reformation from its first impulse to its final consummation. In the very year of his birth Luther fixed his famous theses to the church-door at Wittenburg. Here was the primary step in a movement which spread far and wide, the one overt act from which we may date the commencement of the Reformation throughout Europe. Again, when Bernard Gilpin breathed his last, the plottings of Spain and of the Papacy against England were at their height, plottings which culminated soon after in the Spanish Armada. This may be regarded as the last scene in the great religious drama, as the other was the first. The dispersion of this huge armament, destined for the spiritual and political slavery of England, crowned the work of the Reformation, and set her free to develope her capacities without molestation from foreign tyranny. Looking back on the Reformation from the vantage ground of three centuries, we may criticise the faults without depreciating the blessings. We may deplore the selfishness and greed of some agents; we may mourn over the timidity and inconsistency and time-serving of others; we may lament the extravagances, the shortcomings, of the movement itself. But the fact remains that after every deduction made for these defects, it has been fraught with incomparably great blessings, religious, social, intellectual, political, to England and to the world.

We at least who have lived to see the errors of Rome stereotyped and the tyranny riveted by the promulgation of the doctrine of Papal Infallibility ought not to be insensible to the blessing which fell to England's lot, that three centuries ago England's Church threw off the yoke of the oppressive despotism, that during this period she has developed an independent life, that she has grown with the growth of the English people, and spread with the spread of the English tongue, that she has ramified throughout the known world, and that thus a central standard is erected round which the Churches of the future may rally, and a strong fortress is reared which the growing infidelity of the age will assail in vain. Surely, surely, we shall pour out our hearts in thanksgiving to-day to God, for bestowing upon England and the English Church this His inestimable benefit. If the foundation of the Church is the first cause of thankfulness, the Reformation of the Church must be the second.

3. But thirdly and lastly; we are met together to-day for the special commemoration of one man. If the channel of our thanksgiving is thus narrowed, it will not flow the less fully or strongly on that account. Of all God's gifts to mankind the highest, noblest, most precious is the gift of a saintly example, a saintly life. Such a boon He has bestowed on you, the people of Houghton, in him whom we this

day commemorate. Other parishes in this diocese likewise are linked with his name[78]; but your connexion with him was the longest, the closest, the latest, the most enduring. Here he lived, and here he died. For a whole quarter of a century this parish was the scene of his labours. And as you are his crown of rejoicing, so is he yours. Other rectors not a few you have had, good men and famous men, from age to age; but a fragrance, a beauty, a halo of saintly glory, rests on the name of Bernard Gilpin which rests on none other in the same degree. Houghton is known and honoured for his sake.

A truly good man's career is a rich inheritance for any parish. It propagates by its influence in life, and it fructifies by its example after death. It is a continuous living parable of God's mind and will. It is God's truth translated into action, a book easy to be understood, known and read of all men.

Bernard Gilpin was the true product of the English Reformation, born with its birth, growing with its growth, yielding up his spirit to God at the moment of its consummation. He was its noblest representative also. He appropriated only its excellences, while he was altogether free from its faults. He lost nothing that was valuable in the old, and he apprehended all that was true in the new. Do we enquire what was the secret of this exceptional position? It was his absolute and entire sincerity and unselfishness. He kept his spiritual ear open to God's voice, and therefore God spoke to him. He desired before all things to do God's will, and therefore it was given him to know of the doctrine whether it was of God. He meditated long and seriously over the principles of the Reformation; he went into retirement abroad that he might observe for himself, and ponder by himself; he took every pains to arrive at the truth; he let no worldly interests stand in the way. While the Reformers were in power under Edward, he still clung to the old. When the Roman reaction set in under Mary, he espoused the new.

One feature in his religious life meets us again and again. He was an ardent student of the Scriptures. He did not underrate the value of primitive tradition; but the Bible was his constant companion, his never-failing guide. The Scriptures emancipated him from the errors of Rome.

And he became in his own personal and ministerial life the exponent, the noblest exponent, of the teaching of the Reformation. The changed condition of things required a changed ideal of the pastoral life and work. He was the prototype of the English parish clergyman. Even at this late date, after the lapse of three centuries, he is still the best model on which the priest of the English Church can frame and fashion his life. He anticipated too by three centuries the supplemental work, which in our own age for the first time the clergy have grafted upon their parochial ministrations. He was not only the faithful, earnest, loving rector of Houghton, the father of his flock, but he was likewise the enthusiastic, fearless, impassioned missionary preacher of Tynedale and of Redesdale. His work at home infused his work abroad with sympathy and love; and his work abroad charged his work at home with the fire of zeal. Each acted and reacted on the other.

And in another respect too he was the true exemplar of the English Church. He led the way in that care for education, which happily has (with rare exceptions) been the general characteristic of the English clergy. His grammar-school[79], standing face to face with his church, is a fit emblem of his principles. Religion must go hand in hand with education, that so we may lay on God's altar a higher, fuller, more complete sacrifice of self.

But of the man himself what shall I say? The first feature which strikes us in his character is his absolute disinterestedness, the entire absence of self-seeking, and the complete forgetfulness of worldly advantage, which marked his whole life. Again and again tempting offers are thrown in his way. Again and again they are rejected. They have no temptation for him. It is easier for him to refuse or to resign, than to accept or to retain. 'How tender a thing conscience is,' he wrote on one such occasion, 'I have found by too good experience. I have found, moreover, that as it is easily wounded, so it is with difficulty healed. And for my own part, I speak from my heart, I would rather be often wounded in my body than once in my mind.' In an age of worldliness and self-seeking he was most unworldly.

And allied with his unworldliness is his courage. Witness the spirit which drove him despite all the remonstrances of his friends to return to England a convert to the Reformation when the Marian persecution was raging, and the prospects of the Reformation seemed most hopeless,—to put his head, as it was thought, in the lion's mouth. Witness again his bold denunciation of abuses in the kingdom to his sovereign, and of abuses in the diocese to his bishop. Witness once more his dauntless intervention amidst clashing weapons in that deadly feud of faction and faction in Rothbury church[80].

But unworldliness and courage, when developed in a very high degree, are commonly associated with some weakness or defect of character in the opposite direction. The unworldly man is careless, unmethodical, without capacity in common affairs; the courageous man is hard, exacting, unsympathetic. Bernard Gilpin's character is open to no such charges. We are especially struck with the even balance of his character. No one good quality is developed to the expense of the other. He is bold and fearless, and yet he is tender and loving; he is most unworldly, and yet he shows a business capacity of no common order; he is most profuse in his beneficence, and yet he exercises the strictest and most careful economy. 'I am very much moved concerning him,' said one who came in contact with him in his youth, 'for he doeth and speaketh all things with an upright heart.' 'Cheerfulness,' writes another who lived in our own times, 'cheerfulness was in his soul, because it was in good health. He saw his way through all the paths of life by the lamp of his conscience, which he kept well trimmed. In all things he kept by the model of Christ. Like his Master, he was a sharp sword against the scribes and Pharisees, hypocrites; a place of refuge to the naked and destitute, a shepherd to the flock, food to the hungry, and drink to the thirsty[81].'

This is the man for whose life, for whose influence, for whose memory—far and wide where the English language is spoken, but more especially in this place—we thank God this day. On his death-bed[82], he called the poor people of Houghton about him, and said to them that 'he found that he was going out of the world'; and 'he hoped they would be his witnesses at the Great Day.' 'If ever he had told them any good thing, he would have them remember that in his stead.' Does he not make the same appeal to you their descendants, speaking from yonder grave this afternoon? Yes, be ye his witnesses at the Great Day. If he has taught you any good thing by his life, remember it in your lives. This is the highest and the truest form of commemoration.

Now therefore, we pray thee, dear Lord, grant to us full and grateful hearts that they may overflow with thanksgiving to Thee this day; for that Thou didst purchase a Universal Church by the precious blood of Thy dear Son, and gather it in one from all nations and peoples and tongues; for that in the fulness of time Thou didst through much anguish and many trials purge it from the errors of long centuries; for that Thou didst give to the people of this parish the teaching and example of a heroic and saintly life—an inheritance, a light and a crown of joy to all time.

JOHN COSIN.

PREACHED AT THE REOPENING OF S. PETER'S CHAPEL, AUCKLAND CASTLE.

August 1, 1888.

Thou shalt be called the repairer of the breach, the restorer of paths to dwell in.

ISAIAH lviii. 12.

ON S. Peter's Day, 1665, the building in which we are gathered this morning was consecrated by John Cosin[83], the first bishop after the Restoration. He had been Dean of Peterborough and Master of S. Peter's College; and these two offices which he had borne may have suggested the choice of the day, as well as the dedication of the chapel. Perhaps also, as the ancient parish church of Auckland bears the name of S. Andrew, he may have seen an additional fitness in the choice of his more famous brother, as the Apostle who should give his name to this chapel.

This was not the original destination of the building. Its arcade proclaims its date. It was the ancient hall[84] of the bishop's manor house of Auckland—erected about the middle of the thirteenth century, when the Palatinate was in all its glory. The old chapel had been razed to the ground during the Parliamentary troubles; and Cosin thus supplied its place, removing the ancient roof with its lantern, and throwing up the present clerestory.

This was the crowning act of Cosin's restorations. He had entered the diocese four years before, and had found the material and the spiritual fabrics of the Church alike in dilapidation and disorder, where they were not in complete ruin. At the outbreak of the troubles the aged bishop Morton[85], the most exemplary and blameless of prelates, had been driven from home and office, to seek shelter in the charitable houses of friends, where he lingered on for some years, dying at the advanced age of 95, only a few months before the Restoration.

The Consecration sermon was preached by Cosin's chaplain, Davenport[86]. He was a man of high spiritual aims and generous impulses, notable in many ways. 'When I think,' he wrote to a friend, 'of that burden that was laid on me when I was made a priest, fearfulness and trembling take hold upon me; and in this thing God be merciful to me and to all priests.' It is a thought which will find a response in all our hearts to-day. 'I love a man,' he says in this same letter, 'that loveth the Church as well as his own flesh and blood; and I am of opinion that we priests that have no wives ought to look upon the Church and poor as our next heirs.'

The summer of 1665 was one of the hottest on record, as the summer of 1888 has been one of the coldest. The sweltering heat had nursed and fed the pestilence. The great plague was now at its height in London, and was raging elsewhere in the provinces. On the very day, when the bishop and people were assembled in this chapel for their peaceful celebration, a well-known writer[87] notes in his diary, how at Whitehall he had found 'the court full of waggons and people ready to go out of town.' The plague had attacked the West End with unwonted virulence, and everyone who could was fleeing before the scourge.

The chapel was consecrated, not indeed before such a significant gathering as we witness to-day—an assemblage of bishops gathered from all quarters of the globe[88]—but still before a goodly concourse collected from the diocese itself, 'before the dean and prebendaries and many clergymen,' with 'abundance of gentlemen and gentlewomen.' The preacher took for his text, 'He was worthy for whom he should do this, for he loveth our nation and he has built us a synagogue'—adding significantly the words which follow, 'Then Jesus went with them.' At the close, he tells us, he 'moved all the clergy and laity to be persuaded by the sight of the beauty of this chapel to repair and beautify their own churches and chapels'; nay, he went so far as to 'onerate the conscience' of the bishop and other ecclesiastical officers present 'with the care of seeing it done.'

The period spanned by Cosin's lifetime was pregnant in consequences to the English-speaking people. You in America and in the Colonies, not less than we in England, feel its pulsations vibrating through every part of your political and religious life. The epoch has stamped itself in all its vicissitudes, all its reactions and contradictions, upon us for good or for evil; and the impress will probably last as long as the English race itself.

Two points I would desire especially to emphasize, as having a direct bearing on our meeting to-day.

1. There is first the diffusion of our race, more especially in its religious aspects. Politics were closely bound up with religion—more closely perhaps than at any other epoch in our history. Every political revolution was a religious revolution also. Episcopalian, Presbyterian, Independent, dominated in turn. The vast American continent offered a home to the refugees who could no longer live and worship in peace in the mother country. Thus successive waves of migration swept across the Atlantic, each carrying

its own freight to people the boundless territory which had room for all.

This unhappy alliance of religion with politics was not confined to any one party; nor did it take its rise in the period with which we are concerned. But it was sealed by Laud's compact with absolutism. The divine right of settled, orderly government, as taught by S. Paul, was travestied in the divine right of kings, even of tyrants, as held by Churchmen of the Stuart period. The rude shock, which it received by the Revolution of 1688 and the Non-juring schism[89], was needed to loosen its hold on the mind of the Church. Though you, the members of the American Church, are not responsible for its inception, you have suffered from its effects even more than we. When the independence of the United States was declared, you started heavily weighted in the race. The suspicion which, however unjustly, clung to you and fettered your movements, as the Church of absolutism, the Church of an alien domination, could not be thrown off in a day. Now, thank God, all is changed. It was a happy coincidence, which placed the anniversary of your Declaration of Independence[90] during the session of the Lambeth Conference, and thus enabled us to break up our meeting at an earlier hour that you might pay your respects to your American Minister and exchange congratulations with him on the happy occasion. Your later developments—more especially in those western parts where the injurious tradition inherited from the past had not taken root—are full of hope. Our gathering to-day is an evidence that the Anglican type of Christianity belongs not to any one form of government or any one cast of politics, but can flourish alike under a well-ordered republic and under a constitutional monarchy.

2. This brings me to the second point of which I desire to speak, as the outcome of Cosin's age, and very largely also of Cosin's influence—the type of Christianity which is termed Anglican.

Though it is difficult to define the character of religion and theology in England during the period from the Reformation to the Restoration by any one term, where its manifestations were so various, yet looking at its general tendency we shall not be far wrong in calling it Puritan. It was a reaction—a necessary reaction—from the corruptions of medievalism; and if the pendulum, swinging back, went too far, before it settled in a position of equilibrium, this is the teaching of experience in the moral world as in the physical. The rebound from religious absolutism leads to religious license. The excessive scrupulosity about the externals of religion provokes by a reaction the spirit of irreverence and carelessness.

I would not be mistaken when I use the word

Anglicanism. I desire to guard myself against any narrow interpretation. I believe that the members of the Anglican communion have yet many lessons to learn from medieval Christianity, many also from Puritan Christianity. Can it be otherwise if the type of the true disciple of Christ's kingdom held out in the Gospel—the householder producing from his stores things new and old—is truly apprehended by us? The type of Anglicanism, as it was exhibited in the Caroline era, is too narrow and rigid, too unsympathetic, too deficient in growth and adaptability. Placed as we are amidst the varied activities of an age of exceptional energy, rapid in its movements and manifold in its developments, we ought not to be slow to 'lengthen our cords,' to gather experience, to accumulate spiritual lessons from all sides. Where our opportunities are so great, shall not our acquisitions bear some proportion to them? These Lambeth Conferences, if they did nothing else, ought surely to assist us to this larger conception of Anglicanism; for they gather into a focus the experiences drawn from all lands and from every condition of civilisation and of barbarism.

But, while we 'lengthen our cords,' we must 'strengthen our stakes' likewise. Indeed this strengthening of our stakes will alone enable us to lengthen our cords with safety, when the storms are howling around us. We cannot afford to sacrifice any portion of the faith once delivered to the saints; we cannot surrender for any immediate advantages the threefold ministry which we have inherited from Apostolic times, and which is the historic backbone of the Church. But neither can we on the other hand return to the fables of medievalism or submit to a yoke which our fathers found too grievous to be borne—a yoke now rendered a hundredfold more oppressive to the mind and conscience, weighted as it is by recent and unwarranted impositions of doctrine.

This position was laid down for the English Church at the era of the Restoration. After much swaying to and fro of the religious pendulum, it found rest here. Accusations of Romanism were unscrupulously levelled against Cosin. Nothing could be farther from the truth. During his residence in Paris he was assiduously plied by the Jesuits. The Queen did her best to draw off her English attendants to Romanism. Never was man placed in a position where the temptations to secede were greater. Even his own son was seduced from his allegiance. But Cosin saw his position clearly as a member of the English Church, and he never yielded an inch in the direction of Rome. 'He was the Atlas,' says old Fuller[91], 'of the Protestant religion.' He stood out as the rallying point of the exiled remnant of the Anglican communion, whom he preserved from absorption by his watchfulness and energy. He went even farther than most English Churchmen would go in the present day towards communion with the reformed non-episcopal Churches on the Continent. Even those acts which brought upon him the greatest obloquy and suspicion were done in the interests of the English Church, as against the incentives to Romanism. His book of Devotions[92]—'cozening' devotions, as it was styled by his enemies—was compiled by him, as a counteraction to the Romanist manuals which were offered to the English Court. Whatever else may have been his faults, any leaning to Rome cannot be laid to his charge.

Cosin spent the greater part of his ministerial life in the diocese of Durham. He lived at Auckland before his exile as chaplain, and after his return as bishop. He found this building a hall, and he left it a chapel. Of all places with which his name is connected, none so truly enshrines his life and work, none so fully typifies the career of the English Church in all its vicissitudes during the period of his activity as this. But it especially symbolizes the work of the Restoration, in which he took so active a part.

The Restoration is a subject on which we cannot dwell without much pain. Never had monarch greater opportunities than Charles the Second; never did monarch abuse his opportunities more miserably and shamefully. It is sad also to reflect how much brighter and nobler might have been the future of the English Church, if at this crisis English Churchmen had shown more generosity, more patience and forbearance, more sympathy and love, more of the spirit of Christ towards their opponents. We must hang our heads in shame when we remember that within a few months of the day which saw the consecration of this chapel the cruelty of the Act of Uniformity was whetted to a keener edge by the atrocities of the Conventicles Act and the Five Miles Act. I do not say that comprehension was possible without deserting that position which is the strength of the Anglican Communion as the guardian of primitive truth and of apostolic order against assailants from either side. But if time had been given, if sympathy had been shown, if relief had been afforded, if temporary concessions had been made which might safely have been made, if everything had been done to conciliate in place of exasperating, the loss and discredit to the English Church from the exclusion of so much piety, so much learning, so much conscientious self-sacrifice, on that fatal S. Bartholomew's Day might have been minimised, if it could not have been altogether averted.

But two facts must be borne in mind lest, while we condemn the offence, we do injustice to the offenders.

In the first place, we must remember that it was the age of reprisals. The Anglican clergy did not begin the conflict; they were, at least in most cases, only reinstated in positions which they had held before, and which they regarded as their rightful possession. They had been turned out of house and home; their means of subsistence had been withdrawn; their characters had been blackened; their liturgy had been prohibited; their common worship forbidden. What wonder that, when the turn of the political wheel placed them upmost, they forgot the lessons of forgiveness and charity which the Gospel should have taught them? But it was the misfortune of the English Church that this was the last of the great religious persecutions. Thus it stood out in the memories of men, while its predecessors with all their cruelties were forgotten.

I do not know that Cosin took any active part in carrying these severe measures. I would fain believe not. It is satisfactory at least to find that at the Savoy Conference[93] he is singled out with one other by Baxter, as the two bishops who were willing to make moderate concessions. This not too partial critic describes him as 'of a rustic wit and carriage, so he would endure more freedom of our discourse with him, and was more affable and familiar than the rest.'

In the second place, it should not be forgotten that the laity were at least as eager as the clergy in this sad business. The Houses of Parliament were impatient with the Houses of Convocation. The Commons vied with, and even outstripped, the Lords in the stringency of their measures. Presbyterianism had been discredited in England[94]. 'I know very few or none,' wrote the presbyterian Sharp at this crisis, 'who desire it, much less appear for it.' 'From any observation I can make, I find the Presbyterian cause wholly given up and lost. . . . A knowing minister told me this day, that if a synod should be called by the plurality of incumbents, they would infallibly carry episcopacy. There are many nominal, few real Presbyterians.' To the Independent 'new presbyter' had appeared nothing better than 'old priest writ large.' The Independents themselves had their turn, and were discredited. 'The Restoration,' says a recent writer[95], 'was the work of the whole nation, not of a party. It was the victory of peace, not of loyalty. Men, wearied with confusion, exhausted by strife, frightened by military despotism, sickened by anarchy, turned to the throne and to the Church, because in them they saw not only a protection against disorder but also a guarantee for law.' Alas! that this splendid opportunity was not better used by the victors in the strife.

I do not stand here to praise Cosin at all hazards, though I am standing on his own ground. I could have wished that he had shown less harshness and more sympathy towards the dissenters in his own diocese. I would gladly throw a veil over a certain acerbity of temper, which casts an unlovely hue on his character. But allowance can surely be made to a man, who was driven into exile by the unjust accusations of his enemies—the earliest sufferer in the strife. Much infirmity of temper can be forgiven in one, who laboured under a painful disease, brought on, or at least aggravated, so it was said, by rigorous fasting in his earlier years. But by his strenuous fearlessness, by his great learning, by his unbounded munificence, by his love of order, by his patience and capacity of detail, he did a work, not only for the diocese of Durham, but for the Church of England at large, which she cannot without base ingratitude overlook. When any reproached him with his profuse generosity, which would impair the inheritance of his children, he had his ready reply, 'The Church,' he said, 'is my firstborn.' He was the principal figure among Churchmen in the great drama of the Restoration; and his impress is stamped indelibly on her richest treasure, her Book of Common Prayer.

One lesson more especially of lasting value the Restoration has bequeathed to us, the lesson of hope and confidence. It has shown, as nothing else could have shown, the tough vitality of the Anglican Church. Fuller, addressing his reader five years earlier, writes thus: 'An ingenious gentleman some months since in jest-earnest advised me to make haste with my History of the Church of England, for fear (said he) lest the Church of England be ended before the History thereof.... Blessed be God, the Church of England is still (and long may it be) in being, though disturbed, distempered, distracted; God help and heal her sad condition[96].' The Restoration came, and with it the healing which Fuller desired to see. Yet some years later the king, hearing that Waller the poet intended to give his daughter in marriage to a clergyman, sent to remonstrate with him for marrying her to a falling Church. 'Sir,' replied Waller[97], 'the king does me very great honour to take any notice of my domestic affairs; but I have lived long enough to observe that this falling Church has got a trick of rising again.' The serious and imminent danger at this period was from Romanism—more serious than it has ever been since—Romanism in high places; and the king himself was chiefly responsible for it. This peril too the Church survived. It was this spectre, I presume, looming through the dark mists of the future, which in the life appended to the funeral sermon over Cosin himself suggested the preacher's foreboding utterance, 'Who knows but that God took him away from the evil to come?' *Felix opportunitate mortis!* Happy he, that he did not live to see the betrayal of that Church which he loved so dearly by that family for and with whom he had suffered so much. Again, nearly a century later, the greatest of Cosin's successors, the thoughtful and wise Butler, as is well known, declined the primacy, on the ground that 'it was too late for him to try to support a falling Church[99].' The complaint which prostrated the Church at this time was wholly different from the former. There were no fatal stabs from without; there was no fever or congestion within. The Church seemed dying of atrophy. But she recovered from her prostration, and not only recovered, but started up into a new and vigorous life, of which this concourse to-day is a speaking token. Who could have believed that out of that Church trampled down, crushed, almost annihilated, as it was, under the Commonwealth, out of that poor and withered remnant which was ready to perish, would grow this mighty tree which with its boughs overspreads all lands and all oceans? 'Persecuted, but not forsaken;'

'chastened and not killed;' 'dying, and behold we live.'

From the windows and walls of this chapel[99] more than twelve centuries of history speak to us to-day—the history of the Northumbrian Church, the second cradle of English Christianity. Of all the Churches of Christ since the Day of Pentecost none can produce a purer record of noble work and blameless lives than the early Church of Northumbria—retaining the fragrance and freshness of her Celtic training long after her Celtic teachers had retired. The saints and heroes of this Church—our spiritual ancestors—look down upon us from the windows. There is Oswald, the true-hearted prince, who placed Christ in the forefront of all his endeavours, who would consent to conquer only under the standard of the Cross, whose first care it was, having won back his hereditary kingdom for himself, to win it also for Christ—a true nursing father, not only of the Church of Northumbria but of the Church of England—the prototype of an Alfred and a Louis, of not a few saintly kings throughout the ages. There too is Aidan, the gentlest, simplest, most sympathetic, most loving, most devoted, of missionaries—the rock whence we were hewn—the evangelist to whom before all others the English-speaking peoples owe not this or that benefit, but owe their very selves. There is the royal lady, the saintly Hilda, the mother who arose in our Israel, the messenger of peace in times of distraction and conflict, when every man did what was right in his own eyes, the instructress of bishops and of kings, uniting in herself the wisdom and the capacity of the man with the heart and the sympathy of the woman, diffusing the light of knowledge far and wide. There is the famous Cuthbert, the stripling called like David from the sheep-fold that he might feed the flock of God—the ascetic whose cherished home was the lonely ocean-girt rock and his favourite companions the fowls of the sea—not, it may be, the truest type of saintliness, not the type which would most impress our own age, but a man whose influence was second to none in his own and succeeding generations, and who left an example of self-renunciation which can never die. There is Benedict Biscop, from whose twin houses of Wearmouth and Jarrow the light shone afar, illumining the darkness of the ages with the aurora of our Northern skies, Benedict Biscop who thought no journeys too long and no trouble too great that he might increase the appliances of education and the adornments of the sanctuary—Benedict Biscop who (if he had had no other claim on our remembrance) would have earned our unceasing gratitude as the intellectual and spiritual father of Bede.

There is Bede himself, justly recognised by all succeeding ages as the Venerable, the true impersonation of the scribe instructed into the kingdom of heaven, bringing out of his treasures things new and old, gathering together vast stores of knowledge from every accessible source, and consecrating all to Christ, working on studiously, devotedly, devoutly, to the end, finishing his work only when he finished his life.

These and others second only to these—your spiritual ancestors—look down upon you from the windows; and the history thus begun is continued by the architecture, by the shields, by the records which are imprinted on the building itself—through the middle ages, past the Reformation, over that critical period in the Anglican Church of which I spoke just now, till we reach our own time.

The continuity of our Church in the past is thus unfolded before you. The saints and great ones, though dead, yet speak. The stone cries out of the wall, and the beam out of the timber answers it. The dumb things are vocal of the ages gone by. But what shall I say of our Church in the present—of its diffusion, its achievements, its hopes? Is not this goodly concourse of breathing, acting, speaking men the true response to my question? 'The living, the living, they shall praise Thee, as I do this day.'

'As I do this day.' Yes, whose thanksgiving can be greater than mine—mine who am permitted to welcome you all, my brothers, and to bid you share with me this joyful festival in the dear sanctuary of the home of my fathers? *Quid retribuam Domino?*

JOSEPH BUTLER.

Preached in Durham Cathedral on the Occasion
of his own Enthronement.

May 15, 1879.

And they shall see His face.
REVELATION xxii. 4.

It is related of the greatest of the bishops of Durham that, in his last solemn moments, when the veil of the flesh was even now parting asunder, and the everlasting sanctuary opening before his eyes, he 'expressed it as an awful thing to appear before the Moral Governor of the world[1].'

The same thought, which thus accompanied him in his passage to eternity, had dominated his life in time—this consciousness of an Eternal Presence, this sense of a Supreme Righteousness, this conviction of a Divine Order, shaping, guiding, disposing all the intricate vicissitudes of circumstance and all the little lives of men—enshrouded now in a dark atmosphere of mystery, revealing itself only in glimpses through the rolling clouds of material existence, dimly discerned by the dull and partial vision of finite man, questioned, doubted, denied by many, yet visible enough even now to the eye of faith, working patiently but working surely, vindicating itself ever and again in the long results of time, but awaiting its complete and final vindication in the absolute issues of eternity; the truth of all truths, the reality of all realities, the one stubborn, steadfast fact, unchangeable while all else is changing; this Presence, this Order, this Righteousness, in the language of Holy Scripture this Word of the Lord which shall outlive the solid earth under foot, and the starry vault overhead. 'They shall perish, but Thou remainest, and they all shall wax old as doth a garment; and as a vesture shalt Thou fold them up, and they shall be changed; but Thou art the same, and Thy years shall not fail.' 'All flesh is as grass, and all the glory of man as the flower of grass. The grass withereth, and the flower thereof falleth away; but the word of the Lord endureth for ever.'

It is no arbitrary conjecture that this was the dominating idea of Butler's life. Early and late it is alike prominent in his writings. In the preface to his first great work, his volume of Sermons, he speaks of 'the Author and Cause of all things, Who is more intimately present to us than anything else can be, and with Whom we have a nearer and more constant intercourse than we can have with any creature.' In his latest work, his Charge to the Clergy of Durham, he urges the 'yielding ourselves up to the full influence of the Divine Presence;' he bids his hearers 'endeavour to raise up in the hearts' of their people 'such a sense of God as shall be an habitual, ready principle of reverence, love, gratitude, hope, trust, resignation, and obedience;' he recommends the practice of such devotional exercises 'as would be a recollection that we are in the Divine Presence, and contribute to our being in the fear of the Lord all the day long.' Thus his death-bed utterance was the proper sequel to his lifelong thoughts. The same awe-inspiring, soul-subduing, purifying, sanctifying Presence rose before him as hitherto. But the awe, the solemnity was intensified now, when the vision of God by faith might at any moment give place to the vision of God by sight. Not unfitly did one[2], writing shortly after his decease, compare him to 'the bright lamps before the shrine,' the clear, steady light of the sanctuary, burning night and day before the Eternal Presence.

In the strength of this belief he had lived, and in the awe of this thought he now died. This conviction it was—this sense of a present Righteousness, confronting him always—which raised him high above the level of his age; keeping him pure amidst the surroundings of a dissolute Court; modest and humble in a generation of much pretentious display; high-minded and careless of wealth in a time of gross venality and corruption; firm in the faith amidst a society cankered by scepticism; devout and reverent, where spiritual indifference reigned supreme; candid and thoughtful and temperate, amidst the temptations and the excitements of the religious controversy; careful even for the externals of worship, where such care was vilified as the badge of a degrading superstition. Hence that tremendous seriousness, which is his especial characteristic—that 'awful sense of religion,' that 'sacred horror at men's frivolity' in the language of a living essayist[3]. Hence that transparent sincerity of character, which never fails him. Hence that 'meekness of wisdom,' which he especially urges his clergy to study[4], and of which he himself was all unconsciously the brightest example.

And what more seasonable prayer can you offer for him who addresses you now, at this the most momentous crisis of his life, than that he—the latest successor of Butler—may enter upon the duties of his high and responsible office in the same spirit; that the realisation of this great idea, the realisation of this great fact, may be the constant effort of his life; that glimpses of the invisible Righteousness, of the invisible Grace, of the invisible Glory, may be vouchsafed to him; and that the Eternal Presence, thus haunting him night and day, may rebuke, may deter, may guide, may strengthen, may comfort, may illumine, may consecrate and subdue the feeble and wayward impulses of his own heart to God's holy will and purpose!

And not for the preacher only, but for the hearers also, let the same prayer ascend to the throne of heaven. In all the manifold trials, and all the mean vexations of life, this Presence will be your strength and your stay. Whatsoever is truthful, whatsoever is real, whatsoever is abiding in your lives, if there be any antidote to sin, and if there be any anodyne for grief, if there be any consolation, and if there be any grace, you will find it here and here alone—in the ever-present consciousness that you are living face to face with the Eternal God. Not by fitful gusts of religious passion, not by fervid outbursts of sentimental devotion, not by repetition of approved forms, and not by acquiescence in orthodox beliefs, but by the calm, steady, persistent concentration of the soul on this truth, by the intent fixing of the inward eye on the righteousness and the grace of the Eternal Being before Whom you stand, will you redeem your spirits and sanctify your lives. So will your minds be conformed to His mind. So will your faces reflect the brightness of His face. So will you go from strength to strength, till, life's pilgrimage ended, you appear every one in the eternal Zion, the celestial city, wherein is neither sun nor moon, 'for the glory of God doth lighten it, and the Lamb is the light thereof.'

Let this, then, be the theme of our meditation this morning. Many thoughts will crowd upon our minds, and struggle for utterance, on a day like this; but we will put them all aside. Not our hopes, not our cares, not our burdens, nothing of joy and nothing of sadness, shall interpose now to shut out or to obscure the glory of the Presence before Whom we stand.

Not our hopes; though one hope starts up and shapes itself perforce before our eyes. It will be the prayer of many hearts to-day that the inauguration of a new episcopate may be marked by the creation of a new see; that Northumberland, which in the centuries long past gave to Durham her bishopric, may receive from Durham her due in return in these latest days; that the New Castle on the Tyne may take its place with the Old Castle on the Wear, as a spiritual fortress strong in the warfare of God.

Not our cares; though at this season one anxiety will press heavily on the minds of all. The dense cloud, which for weeks past has darkened the social atmosphere of these northern counties, still hangs sullenly overhead. God grant that the rift, which already we seem to discern, may widen, till the flooding sunlight scatters the darkness, and a lasting harmony is restored to the relations between the employer and the employed.

Not our burdens; though on one at least in this cathedral the sense of a new responsibility must press to-day with a heavy hand. If indeed this burden had been self-sought or self-imposed, if his thoughts were suffered to dwell on himself and his own incapacity, he might well sink under its crushing weight. But your prayer for him, and his ideal for himself, will shape itself in the words which were spoken to the great Israelite restorer of old, 'Not by might, nor by power, but by My Spirit, saith the Lord of Hosts.' Only in this strength before you, as before him, will the great mountain become a plain.

Therefore we will lay down now our hopes and our fears, our every burden, on the steps of the altar; that entering disencumbered into the inmost sanctuary we may fall before the Eternal Presence.

The vision of God is threefold—the vision of Righteousness, the vision of Grace, the vision of Glory.

1. The vision of Righteousness is first in the sequence. Righteousness includes all those attributes which make up the idea of the Supreme Ruler of the universe—perfect justice, perfect truth, perfect purity, perfect moral harmony in all its aspects. Here, then, is the force of Butler's dying words. Ask yourselves,

can it be otherwise than 'an awful thing to appear before the Moral Governor of the world'? You have read perhaps the written record of some pure and saintly life, and you are overwhelmed with shame as you look inward and contrast your sullied heart and your self-seeking aims with his innocency and cleanness of heart. You are confronted—you, an avowedly religious person—in your business affairs, with an upright man of the world; and his straightforward honesty is felt by you as a keen reproach to your disingenuousness and evasion, all the keener because he makes no profession of religion. Yes, you know it; this is the very impress of God's attribute on his soul, though God's name may seldom or never pass his lips. And, if these faint rays of the Eternal Light, thus caught and reflected on the blurred mirrors of human hearts and human lives, so sting and pain the organs of your moral vision, what must it not be then, when you shall stand face to face before the ineffable Righteousness, and see Him in His unclouded glory!

It is a vision indeed of awe, transcending all thought; a vision of awe, but a vision also of purification, of renewal, of energy, of power, of life. Therefore enter into His presence now, and cast yourself down before His throne. Therefore dare to ascend into the holy mountain; dare to speak with God amidst the thunders and the lightnings; dare to look upon the face of His righteousness, that descending from the heights you, like the lawgiver of old, may carry with you the reflexion of His brightness, to illumine and to vivify the common associations and the every-day affairs of life.

Not a few here will doubtless remember how an eloquent living preacher[5] in a striking image employs the distant view of the towers of your own Durham—of my own Durham—seen from the neighbourhood of the busy northern capital only in the clearer atmosphere of Sundays—as an emblem of these glimpses of the Eternal Presence, these intervals of Sabbatical repose and contemplation, when the furnaces and pits cease for the time to pour forth their lurid smoke, and in the unclouded sky the towers of the celestial Zion reveal themselves to the eye of faith. Let this local image give point to our thoughts to-day. 'Unto Thee lift I up mine eyes, O Thou that dwellest in the heavens. Behold, even as the eyes of servants look unto the hand of their masters, and as the eyes of a maiden unto the hand of her mistress, even so our eyes wait upon the Lord our God.'

2. But the vision of Righteousness is succeeded by the vision of Grace. When Butler in his dying moments had expressed his awe at appearing face to face before the Moral Governor of the world, his chaplain, we are told, spoke to him of 'the blood

which cleanseth from all sin.' 'Ah, this is comfortable,' he replied ; and with these words on his lips he gave up his soul to God. The sequence is a necessary sequence. He only has access to the Eternal Love, who has stood face to face with the Eternal Righteousness. He only, who has learned to feel the awe, will be taught to know the grace. The righteous Judge, the Moral Governor of the world, is a loving Father also, is your Father and mine. This is the central lesson of Christianity. Of this He has given us absolute assurance in the life, the death, the words and the works of Christ. The Incarnation of the Son is the mirror of the Father's love. What witness need we more? Happy he who shall realise this fact in all its significance and fulness! Happy he on whom the light of the glory of the Gospel of Christ, Who is the image of God, shall shine; he who shall—

> Gaze one moment on the Face, Whose beauty
>   Wakes the world's great hymn;
> Feel it one unutterable moment
>   Bent in love o'er him ;
> In that look feel heaven, earth, men, and angels,
>   Distant grow and dim;
> In that look feel heaven, earth, men, and angels,
>   Nearer grow through Him[6].

Yes, it is so indeed. All our interests in life, the highest and the lowest alike, abandoned, merged, forgotten in God's love, will come back to us with a distinctness, an intensity, a force, unknown and unsuspected before. Each several outline and each particular hue will stand out in the light of His Grace. Thus we are bidden to lose our souls only that we may find them again. We are charged to give up houses, and brethren, and sisters, and father, and mother, and wife, and children, and lands—all that is lovely and precious in our eyes—to give up all to God, only that we may receive them back from Him a hundredfold, even now in this present time. Our affections, our friendships, our hopes, our business and our pleasure, our intellectual pursuits and our artistic tastes—all our cherished opportunities and all our fondest aims, must be brought to the sanctuary and bathed in the glory of His Presence, that we may take them to us again, baptized and regenerate, purer, higher, more real, more abiding far than before.

3. And thus the vision of love melts into the vision of Glory. So we reach the third and final stage in our progress. This is the crowning promise of the Apocalyptic vision, 'They shall see His face.' The vision is only inchoate now; we catch only glimpses at rare intervals, revealed in the workings of nature and the processes of history, revealed in the lives of God's saints and heroes, revealed above all in the record of the written Word and in the Incarnation of the Divine Son. But then no veil of the flesh shall

dim the vision; no imperfection of the mirror shall blur the image; for we shall see Him face to face—shall see Him as He is—the perfect truth, the perfect righteousness, the perfect purity, the perfect love, the perfect light. And we shall gaze with unblenching eye, and our visage shall be changed. Not now with transient gleam of radiance, as on the lawgiver of old, shall the light be reflected from us; but, resting upon us with its own ineffable glory, the awful effluence—

> Shall flood our being round, and take our lives
> Into itself.

Of this final goal of our aspirations, of this crowning mystery of our being, the mind is helpless to conceive, and the tongue refuses to tell. Silent contemplation, and wondering awe, and fervent thanksgiving alone befit the theme. Even the inspired lips of an Apostle are hushed before it. 'Beloved, now are we the sons of God, and it doth not yet appear what we shall be; but we know that, when He shall appear, we shall be like Him, for we shall see Him as He is'—we shall see Him as He is.

APPENDIX.

Preached by the Right Reverend Brooke Foss Westcott, D.D., D.C.L., Lord Bishop of Durham, at the consecration of S. Columba's Church, Southwick, Sunderland.

June 9, 1890.

They that seek the Lord shall not want any good thing.
PSALM xxxiv. 10.

SUCH were the last words which Columba wrote on the eve of his death. 'Here,' he said, when he finished the verse as he was transcribing the Psalter, 'I must stop at the close of the page; my scholar shall write what follows.' And most truly his biographer adds, 'This verse was appropriate to the master as the next was to the disciple—"Come ye children, hearken unto me, I will teach you the fear of the Lord."' Brethren, we hearken now and seek to learn the lesson while our thoughts go back to that early morning nearly 1,300 years ago, when, as on this day, the promise found fulfilment on the desolate shore of Iona, and the teaching of a life of sacrifice was consummated.

The death of Columba was a true revelation of

the saint. Twice, as it is related, the time of his departure had been delayed; once through the prayers of the churches that his help might still be continued to them, and once by his own prayer that his decease might not disturb the joy of Easter. But at last his Sabbath, his rest-day, as he called it, which he had foreseen, drew near. He knew that he must render to God on the morrow the life which had been entrusted to him. With tender thought for his household he went to the monastery barn and blessed it, and thanked God that his monks had still a year's supply in store. Afterwards he climbed the little knoll which overlooked the monastery itself, and blessed his house, and foretold how kings of foreign lands and saints of other Churches should do reverence to the mean and lowly place; then he returned to his own poor hut and continued a work of his early days, a transcription of the Psalter, till he paused at the words I have taken for my text. The evening service then followed; after this he went to rest, with a bare rock, as Adamnan says, for straw, and a stone for his pillow. So resting he gave his parting counsel. 'These, my little children,' he said, 'are my last words. I charge you to keep unfeigned love one with another. If you do so after the pattern of the fathers, God, the champion of the good, will help you...' At midnight the bell sounded for matins.

Columba sprang up and entering the church before any of the brethren fell on his knees before the altar. A faithful attendant followed, and saw from afar the whole church flooded with angelic light. When he came to the door the light vanished; but groping his way through the darkness, he found the saint and lifted up his head and placed it in his bosom. By this time the brethren had come in with lights, and burst into lamentation at the sight of their dying master. Columba opened his eyes and looked round with an expression of marvellous gladness, for (his biographer adds) he saw the angel who had come to meet him, and responding to the action of his friend he feebly raised his hand that he might give by a sign the benediction which he could not pronounce with his failing breath. And so, like his Lord, he passed away in blessing.

The scene rises vividly before us, after the long centuries, with an unchanged and unchangeable message of victorious devotion. The hope, the prophecy of Columba still find fulfilment. He is to-day a living Evangelist on the crowded banks of the Wear, among people of another tongue, as on the desolate rocks of the place of his chosen exile. In different forms, under strange varieties of circumstance, his influence has found scope in this distant country. When Oswald was preparing himself for what seemed to be a desperate conflict, Columba, it is said, appeared to him in a vision and with cheering words nerved him for victory. The cathedral at Durham claimed to possess among its treasures some of his relics; and now in our latest age a church is raised here to bear his name and bring, as we trust, something of his spirit among us, a spirit purified by the discipline of great sorrows in the power of peace.

We desire to honour the memory of Columba, and happily his portrait has been preserved to us in a life by Adamnan, which has justly been described as 'the most complete piece of such biography which Europe can boast of' to the end of the middle ages. In this we see him as he appeared to those among whom he moved, and we can realise, at least in the broad features, what he was. He was then, in a word, a true man; a true Irishman; with all the virtues and faults of his race; tender, affectionate, self-willed, imperious, even fierce. The words of the Psalmist seem to find expression in his actions: 'How do I hate them, O Lord, that hate Thee.' He was not perfect, but he was a saint, complete, not in faultlessness, but in the unreserved consecration of his whole nature.

When we go further into detail we are guided by the plan of his biographer, who has grouped the memorials of Columba's life under three divisions:

his prophecies, his miracles, his visions. By this arrangement he has rightly distinguished Columba's three main characteristics: his power of penetrative sympathy, his love of nature, his depth of spiritual insight. Columba read the heart of man, and therefore he could divine its issues. He felt the unity of creation, and therefore he could decipher some mysteries of its life. He saw the Presence of God, and therefore he could reflect its light. So, reading, feeling, seeing, he mastered, little by little, through struggles and losses, the lesson which we must try to learn, the lesson which he bequeathed at his death, the lesson of trust and peace.

I. Columba, I say, loved men, and through love he understood them. He was enabled to recognise the signs of a divine kinsmanship, the unconscious strivings after noble things, in the ignorant, the rude, the wayward. On one occasion when he was visiting the monastery of Clonmacnoise, a poor serving boy, mean, unpopular, and despised, sought, like the woman in the Gospel, to touch secretly from behind the hem of his garment. The saint perceived his purpose and laid his hand upon him and set him before him. The bystanders prayed him to loose hold of the wretched creature. 'Suffer it to be so now,' he replied, and bade the trembling boy open his mouth and put out his tongue. Thereupon he blessed him, and said to the astonished company, 'Let no man despise him however vile he may seem. From this hour he shall grow in favour and worth and wisdom, and his tongue shall be the organ of Divine eloquence.' The words found fulfilment and the lad grew up to be a saint, famous through all the churches of Ireland.

It is no wonder, therefore, that, gifted with this spiritual discernment, this sovereign hope, he claimed the obedience of complete devotion.

'You cannot stay with me a year,' he said to two pilgrims, who begged to be received for a time, 'unless first you take the monastic vow.' 'Though we had no such purpose,' was the reply, 'we yield to a word that must be inspired.' And when the brethren marvelled that poor unknown wanderers were so received without trial, Columba answered, 'These two strangers by their willing self-sacrifice have fulfilled their Christian warfare, and both shall pass away in peace within the month.' Columba had traced in them with the unerring instinct of the artist or physician the signs of death, and with the insight of an apostle the capacity for saving faith, and he used his knowledge for the love of Christ.

Such examples illustrate Columba's power. By a living sympathy he entered into the souls of those who came before him. He knew, as it has been well said, how 'to be poor of heart among the poor, how to weep for those who would not weep for themselves;' he knew how to foresee the bitter end of ostentatious austerities and the victory of humble penitence; how to bring peace by homely wisdom to a divided household; how to recognise the promise of a divine blessing in the willing accomplishment of the natural law written in man's heart. He had mastered the secret of effective help to the suffering by making his own the burden of which they could be relieved. On a bitter winter's day the saint was seen weeping. 'It is not strange that I should be distressed,' he replied to those who asked the cause, 'for I see my monks toiling far off at Durrow in a grievous case.' And forthwith, it is said, their taskmaster, stung by some sudden impulse, set them free and gave them necessary refreshment. We may lay the lesson to heart. Perhaps we have not yet learnt how soul touches soul, how prayer works its effects naturally, as we speak, through sympathy; and I seem able to understand how the tired reapers at Iona, when they returned home in the evening, found their loads lightened, as we read, when they reached the most difficult part of their way, for then Columba went to meet them in spirit, as he could not cheer them by his bodily presence.

II. Columba loved men, and he loved nature

also, and through his love he was enabled to master some of the secrets of that deeper life which lies beneath material things.

> 'For nature never did betray
> The soul that loved her.'

Even if a strict criticism throws doubt upon the authorship of the Irish poems which are attributed to him, these show at least what he was supposed to feel. And nowhere can we find more vivid images brought together, 'the song of the wonderful birds,' 'the thunder of the crowding waves,' 'the level sparkling strand,' all summoned before the eyes of the singer's heart that he may better bless the Lord —that is the end of all—in prayer, and praise, and meditation, and work, and almsgiving.

So Columba, like many other early saints, learnt the truth that

> 'He prayeth well who loveth well,
> Both man, and bird, and beast.'

And there is no more characteristic story of his tenderness than that which tells how he bade one of his brethren watch by the western shore of the island in order to receive, and cherish, and feed a wayworn crane which would be driven there by the winds and fall exhausted at his feet. 'It comes,' he pathetically said, 'from our own fatherland.' He had measured, we see, the effects of the storm, and thought of the sufferings of the humblest creature which he could help. And so in the narrative of his death it is told that when he rested for a little while on his last return to his cabin, a faithful horse came up to him and placed his head in his lap, and wept like a man. 'You,' the saint said to the servant, who would have driven the beast away, 'with all your reason could not foresee my departure, but the Creator has revealed it to this poor brute in such a way as pleased Him.'

III. Columba loved men and he loved nature because in both he saw God. His vision embraced the great spiritual realities of life. He regarded things with a spiritual eye: therefore his countenance flashed from time to time with beams of an unearthly joy, when, in the language of his biographer, he saw the ministering angels round about him. Nor can we forget the truth which lies in the imagery. The first great promise in the Gospel assures us of the renewed intercourse between earth and heaven. 'Ye shall see,' the Lord said, using for the first time the title by which He is bound with the race, 'the heavens opened and the angels of God ascending and descending upon the Son of Man.' For us in virtue of the Incarnation, that which was shown to the patriarch in a vision has become a fact; and if we are told to see the angels ascending first, is it not that we may recognise the presence of the unseen powers among whom we live, whether we notice them or not? For Columba himself nothing was without the care of God: he trained his disciples to his faith, and they answered to his discipline. When a favourite scholar proposed to cross to a neighbouring island the saint told him, trying him, as we may suppose, of the monstrous creature that had been just now seen in the mid-channel. 'I and that beast,' was the reply, 'are under the power of God.' 'Go in peace,' the master then said, 'thy faith in Christ shall defend thee from this peril.' 'Follow me not,' he said to another, 'thou mayest not abandon father, and mother, and country.' 'Thou art my father,' was the answer, 'and the Church is my mother, and my country is where I can gather the largest harvest for Christ.'

Through such traits we can in some way realise the man, unsparing of others as of himself, demanding the absolute self-surrender he had made, open-eyed, to the world, in all its rich variety of changing phenomena, yet passionately fond of the written Scriptures; a sign to all who looked on him of the energy of spiritual forces, as he wielded the powers of the age to come.

What then, we ask, does Columba mean for us, this keen impulsive conqueror of souls, fearless in perils and restless in labour? Even in the simplest sense, we need the inspiration of his example in the strain of our conventional life. We need his bold trust in humanity, his confident appeal to generous feelings, his courageous exercise of moral supremacy, his strengthening of the family when he made the ties of the clan the model of his own order. We need his reverence for what we speak of as lower forms of life, the gentle love with which he confessed in deed that He who made him made them too; the thankfulness with which he acknowledged that life lies not in the things which we possess, out of their superfluous abundance, but in the splendours of earth and sky, and the joys of human intercourse, and the consciousness of divine kinsmanship, which are our common heritage. We need above all the power of spiritual vision, which discerns the eternal in things transitory, the terrible issues of self-assertion, the joy of consecrated service; a vision which is sufficient to chasten, to cheer, to inspire, to elevate, the simplest routine of daily duties.

What does Columba mean for us? To answer this question more fully here we must take account of the sister Church across the stream. Columba of Hy, Ignatius of Antioch; Columba, the Celtic missionary, and Ignatius, the Syrian martyr, honoured alike among us, symbolise the catholicity of our own

Church. By a happy choice the very buildings in which they are commemorated are not less widely separated in type than are the men themselves. Here we have the Basilica representing the energy of that Roman law by which the Christian civilization of the West was united with the past; and on the other side the purest forms of Gothic architecture in which the Faith found its own natural expression in the North. And it is not, I think, an idle fancy which gladly notes that the very contrasts are combined in another contrast. The Roman sanctuary is assigned to the Irish saint and the English sanctuary to the Eastern one. Separately and together, sanctuary and saint, remind us of that which is our joy and our hope, that no one outward form, no one national character, no one man, can exhaust the fulness of our faith.

Here in this church the thought lies embedded for ever in the very foundations of the building. The foundation stone itself is two stones and not one stone: in that Irish and English are cemented together; and this material union will force all who worship here to think of and to pray for that consummation when every division of race and class shall be done away, and all whom Christ has redeemed shall be one man in Him.

All our hearts beat quicker when we think of such

a consummation; but in order that we may share and enjoy and strengthen the spirit of catholicity which springs out of loyal devotion to a living Lord, whereby it is hastened, we must be prepared to give up much that we severally hold dear. God will bless the offering of our private preferences, habits, convictions, if it is made for a greater cause. It has been often said that there is nothing fruitful but sacrifice. I will dare to add that there is no lasting strength without obedience. Thus it may be that through the discipline of trial we shall ourselves find opportunities in the present perils which we view with the greatest alarm. The very work of Columba was the penitent confession of a great fault, the transfiguration of a great sorrow.

What does Columba mean for us, for me, to-day? The saint who stirs us after thirteen centuries with fresh enthusiasm, who speaks to us, though dead, with a voice of warning and encouragement, who helps us to reach out to the breadth and manifoldness of our faith, is recognised as a living friend. So God enables us to feel that earthly connexions are not essential to a true human fellowship. And such a reflexion cannot but stir us deeply here and now. The very form of our service tells us of one no longer seen whose presence is in all our hearts, and my own thoughts necessarily go back to words spoken not yet a year ago, words of thankfulness and hope, when your loved Father in God was given back, as we trusted, for a fresh period of faithful work. I do not wish to retract or to modify one phrase of joy and confidence which I used then. The gift has been made otherwise than we expected. But the gift is real and it is abiding. Never was the influence of him whom we have rather found than lost—I speak from daily experience—more powerful or more salutary; never did the sense of his absolute singleness of purpose constrain his people to bend their energies to one common end with surer effect; never was his strong wisdom more powerful to commend to our hearts the grace of fellowship, than now, when he moves us with a force from which all admixture of transitory elements is for ever taken away. It is through the saints of God, when their image rises before our soul in its purity, that we learn to recognise what is great and what is little in life: learn to distinguish what survives in glory through the last momentous change: learn to discern, dimly it may be and far off, that unity in which we find the co-ordination of our several activities, the completion of our fragmentary thoughts.

Yet once again, What does Columba mean for us? The answer which is addressed to all time, wrought out through his life, lies in the last words which he wrote and the last charge which he gave. This is his testament, 'They that seek the Lord shall not want any good thing.' 'My little children, keep unfeigned love one with another.' The promise is accomplished through every variety of outward circumstance. The command is valid through every temptation of personal differences. If we bear the promise and the command in our memory, as we all can do; if we ponder them; if we bring them to the interpretation of our disappointments and our trials, it will not have been in vain that we have dwelt for a short space on the teaching of the first forefather of our Northern Church. Hear him then once more; hear psalmist and apostle through him: 'They that seek the Lord shall not want any good thing.' 'My little children, keep unfeigned love one with another.'

NOTES.

NOTES.

1. S. COLUMBA was born of royal descent at Gartan in Donegal on Dec. 7, 520 or 521. Educated under the two Finnians and others, he was in due time ordained deacon and priest, but never raised to the episcopate. He taught at Glasnevin near Dublin until the plague broke up the school in 544, when he returned to the north of Ireland, and founded numerous monasteries, the most important of which were Durrow (Dearmach), Derry and Kells. Dr Reeves enumerates thirty-seven of these foundations in Ireland. The actual circumstances which led to his leaving his native country are variously given. The best-known story is as follows. In his enthusiasm for manuscripts he had secretly copied a Psalter belonging to Finnian, who thereupon claimed the copy as his own. The matter was referred to king Diarmid, Columba's kinsman, at Tara, who decided in favour of Finnian, saying: 'To every cow her calf; so to every book its copy.' Offended at this decision Columba stirred up the families of the north Hy Neills against the south Hy Neills who acknowledged Diarmid, and the result was the defeat of Diarmid, owing to the prayers and songs of Columba. Columba's Latin copy of the Psalter became the national relic of the O'Donnell clan, and for a thousand years was carried with them to battle. It is still preserved, and from its date may well have been written by the saint. But whatever was the immediate cause of quarrel, it seems certain that the battle of Cooldrevny (Coledebrina) fought in 561 between the Hy Neills was attributed in a great measure to Columba's influence.

A synod held at Teltown in Meath censured his conduct, though apparently it did not excommunicate him. Stung with remorse, he sailed from Ireland with twelve companions, a voluntary exile for the cause of Christ (*pro Christo peregrinari volens enavigavit*, Adamnan pref. 2), and settled in the island of Iona (Hy) in the year 563 (see

Reeves' *Life of S. Columba*; Bede *H. E.* iii. 4 gives it 565). Here he founded his chief monastery, and evangelised the heathen Picts. He also taught more carefully the Scots, who had already been converted to Christianity by S. Ninian. For thirty-five years S. Columba laboured with wonderful energy, travelling through great parts of Scotland, and penetrating northward as far as Inverness, and eastward into Aberdeenshire, founding churches, and monastic institutions, among others the famous monastery of Deer. He frequently visited Ireland on matters connected with his monasteries, which he superintended until the end.

The circumstances of his death are very touching. On the Saturday afternoon he was transcribing the thirty-third Psalm. He reached the verse, 'They who seek the Lord shall want no manner of thing that is good,' and then said, 'Here I must stop; what follows let Baithen write.' As the midnight bell summoned the brethren to the matins of the Sunday festival he hastened before the other monks to the chapel. When lights were brought, they found him prostrate before the altar, and in the act of blessing them he passed away with a smile upon his face, 'doubtless seeing the holy angels coming to meet him.' This according to Dr Reeves' computation was early in the morning of Sunday, June 9, A.D. 597.

The chief authority for the life of S. Columba is his biography by Adamnan, ninth abbot of Iona, written between 692 and 697 (edited by Reeves Dublin 1857). See also Bede *Hist. Eccl.* iii. 4, Montalembert *Monks of the West* iii. p. 97 sq. (Engl. trans.), and especially Reeves' *Life of S. Columba* in *Historians of Scotland* Vol. VI.

2. This devoted follower was Mochonna, son of the provincial king of Ulster. 'In vain Columba represented to him that he ought not to abandon his parents and native soil. "It is thou," answered the young man, "who art my father, the Church is my mother, and my country is where I can gather the largest harvest for Christ." Then, in order to render all resistance impossible, he made a solemn vow aloud to leave his country and follow Columba, "I swear to follow thee wherever thou goest, until thou hast led me to Christ, to whom thou hast consecrated me."' Montalembert *Monks of the West* iii. p. 132.

3. 'It was the general belief of the time that all islands fell under the jurisdiction of the Papal See, and it was as a possession of the Roman Church that Henry sought Hadrian's permission to enter Ireland. His aim was "to enlarge the bounds of the Church, to restrain the progress of vices, to correct the manners of its people and to plant virtue among them, and to increase the Christian religion." He engaged to "subject the people to laws, to extirpate vicious customs, to respect the rights of the native Churches, and to enforce the payment of Peter's pence" as a recognition of the overlordship of the Roman See. Hadrian by his bull approved the enterprize as one prompted by "the ardour of faith and love of religion," and declared his will that the people of Ireland should receive Henry with all honour, and revere him as their lord.' Green *History of the English People* i. 176. Hadrian IV (Nicholas Breakespeare), a native of S. Albans and the antagonist of Frederick Barbarossa, was pope from 1154 to 1159 (Milman *Latin Christianity* Book VIII. ch. 7).

4. On the influence of S. Columban (543—615) and his Celtic followers upon the evangelisation of Europe see Montalembert *Monks of the West* ii. p. 387 sq, Neander *Church History* v. p. 39 sq. He preached in France, Switzerland and Italy. His principal monasteries were Luxeuil in the Vosges, and Bobbio near Milan. St Gall on Lake Constance was founded and named after his companion Gallus. S. Columban first gave the impulse to the missionary enterprise in England and Ireland which produced Cilian, Wilfrid, Willibrord, Willibald, Winfrid (Boniface) and many others.

5. Paulinus was one of four monks sent from Rome by Gregory the Great in 601 to recruit the mission of Augustine. In 625 he was chosen to accompany as chaplain Ethelburga, daughter of Eadbald, king of Kent, when she went to be bride to Edwin, king of Northumbria; and he was consecrated bishop of York by Justus, archbishop of Canterbury. Though allowed free exercise of his religion, he made little or no impression on king or court, until the escape of Edwin from an assassin's dagger on Easter-eve 626, and the birth to him of a daughter the same night, were taken advantage of by Paulinus to direct his attention to Christianity. Edwin allowed the infant to be baptized at Pentecost, but with characteristic caution hesitated to embrace the faith; and it was not until the following winter that he summoned his Witan at Goodmanham to listen to the preaching of Paulinus. The effect of the conference was immediate: Coifi, the chief Pagan priest, took the lead in the desecration of the heathen shrine at Goodmanham: on Easter-eve 627, in a wooden chapel erected for that purpose at York on the site of the present Minster, Edwin and his nobles were baptized, and the impulse thus given to Christianity was felt through the length and breadth of the great kingdom of Northumbria. Everywhere crowds flocked to receive baptism at Paulinus' hands.

The Glen in Northumberland, the Derwent in Durham, the Eure and the Swale in Yorkshire are rivers associated with his missionary journeys. Pallinsburn, some three miles from the Tweed near the well-known field of Flodden, preserves his name. His traditional well at Holystone, in the Coquet valley, is still shown. He even penetrated as far south as Lindsey, then subject to Northumbria, and preached at Lincoln; and there he consecrated Honorius to be fifth archbishop of Canterbury. But he appears to have taken no steps to organize his work. The results, though brilliant, were superficial, and when the defeat and death of Edwin at Hatfield (Oct. 12, 633) were followed by the cruel devastation of Northumbria by Penda and Cadwalla, he felt that Christianity was a lost cause, abandoned his bishopric, and set sail with the widowed Ethelburga for Kent, where archbishop Honorius and king Eadbald gave him the see of Rochester. Next autumn arrived from Rome the pall intended for him as archbishop of York in accordance with Gregory's original scheme for two archbishoprics in England each with twelve suffragan bishops. But it came too late: and so Paulinus was never archbishop. He died bishop of Rochester Oct. 10, 644, and was buried in the chapter-house there. See Bede *Hist. Eccl.* i. 29; ii. 9, 12—14, 16—18, 20; iii. 1, 14.

6. Nullum fidei Christianae signum, nulla ecclesia, nullum altare in tota Berniciorum gente erectum est, priusquam hoc sacrae crucis vexillum novus militiae ductor, dictante fidei devotione, contra hostem immanissimum pugnaturus statueret. Bede *Hist. Eccl.* iii. 2.

7. Montalembert *Monks of the West* iv. p. 88.

8. Montalembert *Monks of the West* iv. p. 125.

9. Montalembert *Monks of the West* iv. p. 126.

10. Habere autem solet ipsa insula rectorem semper abbatem presbyterum, cujus juri et omnis provincia, et ipsi etiam episcopi, ordine inusitato, debeant esse subjecti, juxta exemplum primi doctoris illius, qui non episcopus, sed presbyter extitit et monachus (Moreover, the island itself is wont to have always an abbot, who is a presbyter, for its ruler, to whose jurisdiction all the province and the bishops also themselves, after an unusual order, are bound to be subject, according to the example of their famous first teacher, who was not a bishop, but a presbyter and a monk) Bede *Hist. Eccl.* iii. 4. See also Bright *Early English Church History* (2nd edition) p. 139 sq.

11. The three forms of tonsure were (1) the Roman (S. Peter's) 'the hair shorn away from the top of the head in a circular shape more or less wide, according as the wearer happened to be high or low in order : the hair clipt over the ears and all about the neck in such a way, that from behind and on the sides it looked like a ring or crown around the head;' (2) the Celtic 'made by cutting away the hair from the upper part of the forehead in the figure of a half-moon, with the convex side before;' (3) the Greek (S. Paul's) the shaving of the whole head. Great importance was attached to the form of tonsure. Theodore of Tarsus when nominated archbishop of Canterbury 'waited four months' in Rome 'until his hair should be grown, so that it might be shorn in the shape of a crown. For he had had the tonsure of the holy apostle Paul, after the manner of the Easterns (quatuor exspectavit menses, donec illi coma cresceret, quo in coronam tonderi posset ; habuerat enim tonsuram more orientalium sancti apostoli Pauli)' Bede *Hist. Eccl.* iv. 1. The Celtic tonsure was nicknamed by its opponents 'the tonsure of Simon Magus' (Bede *Hist. Eccl.* v. 21). See Mayor and Lumby *Bede* p. 293 sq.

The question of the keeping of Easter was a more intricate one. There was no dispute as to the day of the week, for, like the Roman, the Celtic Church kept the festival always on a Sunday. The Celtic Church therefore was never Quartodeciman, and Colman's appeal at the Council of Whitby to the precedent of S. John was rightly disproved by Wilfrid. The difference between the usages was twofold ; (1) in calculating the date of Easter, the Celtic Churches used an antiquated and imperfect Paschal Calendar, which elsewhere had been superseded by a more accurate reckoning ; (2) the Celtic Church allowed Easter day to fall on the fourteenth day of the moon, the Roman Church never before the fifteenth day. Eanfleda, Oswy's queen, who had been brought up in Kent, observed the Roman usage ; hence, as Bede tells us (*Hist. Eccl.* iii. 25) 'it sometimes happened in those times that the paschal feast was kept twice in one year ; and when the king, having ended his fast, was keeping the Lord's paschal feast, the queen with her court still continuing in her fast was keeping Palm Sunday.' See further in Bright, pp. 79 sq., 202 sq.

12. The Council of Whitby (Streanæshalch) was held in the spring of 664 to settle these points. Colman, bishop of Lindisfarne, Hilda, abbess of Whitby, Cedd, bishop of the East-Saxons (then on a visit to Lastingham) represented the Celtic usage, to which king Oswy also inclined : queen Eanfleda, her son, prince Alchfrid, Agilbert the Frank, bishop of Dorchester, James the Deacon, a survivor of the mission of Paulinus, Tuda, an Irish bishop recently arrived in Northumbria, and above all, Wilfrid, abbot of Ripon, supported the Roman view. King Oswy presided, and when Colman had spoken in favour of the customs of Lindisfarne called upon Agilbert on the other side. He not being able to speak Saxon requested that his disciple Wilfrid might be spokesman on his behalf. Thereupon Wilfrid, whose visits to France and Rome gave him a great advantage over his opponents, had little difficulty in disposing of the arguments of Colman. The end of the debate was remarkable. Colman, after his appeal to S. John had been disproved, had quoted in support of his view Anatolius and Columba. Wilfrid replied, 'Even if your Columba,—let me say *ours* if he was Christ's—was a saint and a wonder worker, ought he therefore to be preferred to the most blessed chief of the apostles, to whom the Lord said, "Thou art Peter, and upon this rock I will build My Church, and the gates of hell shall not prevail against it: and I will give thee the keys of the kingdom of heaven?"' King Oswy was much impressed by this reference. He asked Colman whether the words were really spoken by Christ to S. Peter? 'Certainly.' 'Did He ever give the like power to your Columba?' 'No.' 'You both agree that these words were said especially to Peter, and that the keys of heaven were given him by the Lord.' 'Yes,' they both said, 'certainly.' 'And I tell you, that this is that doorkeeper, whom I choose not to contradict, but as far as I know or am able, I desire in all things to obey his rulings; lest perchance when I come to the doors of the kingdom of heaven, I may find none to unbar them for me, if he be averse who is proved to hold the keys.' And with that he decided against the Celtic party. Colman retired first to Iona, afterwards to Inisboffin, an island off the coast of Mayo, leaving Eata, abbot of Melrose, formerly one of Aidan's 'twelve boys,' to rule, as abbot, over those of his brethren who preferred to remain behind at Lindisfarne. See Bede *Hist. Eccl.* iii. 25, 26.

13. Montalembert *Monks of the West* iv. p. 170.

14. See the panegyric of Bede (*Hist. Eccl.* iii. 26), a summary of which is given in Montalembert *Monks of the West* iv. 22 sq.

15. In 675, when contemplating the monastery of Wearmouth, Benedict Biscop brings back from Gaul 'masons to erect a church in the Roman style, which he had always admired (caementarios qui lapideam sibi ecclesiam juxta Romanorum, quem semper amabat, morem facerent).' Bede *Vitae B. Abbatum* 5. At Ripon and Hexham Wilfrid erected stone churches of great magnificence. In 710 we find Naiton (Nectan), king of the Picts, sending to Ceolfrid, abbot of Jarrow, for 'architects to build a church of stone in his nation in the Roman style (architectos petiit qui juxta morem Romanorum ecclesiam de lapide in gente ipsius facerent)' Bede *Hist. Eccl.* v. 21.

16. On the Pseudo-Isidorian Decretals see Neander *Church History* (Torrey's translation) vi. p. 1 sq. A collection of ecclesiastical laws had been drawn up in the sixth century by Dionysius Exiguus containing the papal decrees from the time of Pope Siricius (384—398) downwards. This collection was widely circulated, and was added to from time to time by the admission of later ecclesiastical ordinances. One of the best known of these recensions was that of the learned Isidore of Seville (560—636). But in the ninth century suddenly appeared, under the name of Isidore, a collection no longer commencing from the fourth century, but comprising a complete series of decretals of the Roman bishops from Clement of Rome (c. 92—100) onwards. It was headed by five letters purporting to have been written by Clement, of which one was a Latin translation by Rufinus (c. 398—402) of a spurious letter to James, which is found in Greek prefixed to the Clementine Homilies, a work of the second century; the others later fabrications. The letters from subsequent bishops of Rome in this collection abound in anachronisms and blunders of such a kind that a less credulous age would have detected the imposture at once; and the whole series was designed to set forth in the completest way, and to invest with the authority of great antiquity, the inviolability of the Church, and the claim of the Pope, as the head of Christendom, to be the sole court of appeal in civil and religious matters alike.

17. John, surnamed the Faster, patriarch of Constantinople (585—595) had assumed the title of 'oecumenical' or 'universal' bishop in the time of Pelagius, Gregory's predecessor. The title was not a novelty, nor did it apparently imply a claim for jurisdiction over the whole church; but Gregory remonstrated strongly in his letters. Writing to the emperor Maurice he declares (Ep. vii. 33), Ego fidenter dico quia quisquis se universalem episcopum vocat, vel vocari desiderat, in electione sua Antichristum praecurrit, quia superbiendo se caeteris proponit. Nec dispari superbia ad errorem ducitur quia, sicut perversus ille deus videri vult super omnes homines, ita quisquis iste est, qui solus sacerdos appellari appetit, super reliquos sacerdotes se extollit (I say confidently that whoever styles himself 'universal bishop,' or seeks to be so styled, becomes by his own choice a precursor of Antichrist; because by his proud vaunting he places himself above the rest. In a like spirit of pride he is being led away into error; for just as that false god wishes to seem superior to all men, so whoever this person is, who covets to be called priest all to himself, he exalts himself above his fellow priests). Again in a letter addressed to Eusebius, bishop of Thessalonica and other bishops (Ep. ix. 60), after an allusion to superbum et pestiferum oecumenici, id est universalis, vocabulum (the proud and pestilent title of 'oecumenical' or 'universal'), he continues, Quia hoc jam, ut videmus, mundi hujus termino propinquante, in praecursione sua apparuit humani generis inimicus, ut ipsos, qui ei contradicere bene atque humiliter vivendo debuerunt per hoc superbiae vocabulum praecursores habeat sacerdotes, hortor et suadeo ut nullus vestrum hoc nomen aliquando recipiat (Since therefore with the end of this world approaching, as we see, in his due time of forerunning has appeared the enemy of the human race, so as to have as his precursors the very men who ought to have given him the lie by living good and humble lives, the priests, I advise and urge that none of you on any account admit this title). And later on in the same letter, Quis, rogo, in hoc tam perverso vocabulo nisi ille ad imitandum proponitur, qui, despectis angelorum legionibus secum sociabiliter constitutis, ad culmen conatus est singularitatis erumpere, ut et nulli subesse et solus omnibus praeesse videretur (Who, I ask, in this preposterous title is held up for imitation but he who despised the legions of angels which had been associated with himself on equal terms, and essayed to force his way to the topmost point of singularity, so that he might appear not merely inferior to none, but sole head above all)? Many equally strong passages might be quoted from Ep. v. 18, 20, 43; vii. 31, 33; viii. 30, ix. 68. See Robertson *History of the Christian Church* ii. 376 sq.

18. Tennyson *The Passing of Arthur* l. 183.

19. Finan, the successor of S. Aidan and the predecessor of Colman in the bishopric of Lindisfarne (651—661), built the church at Lindisfarne 'after the manner of the Scots (Celts), not of stone but entirely of hewn oak, and thatched it with reeds (more Scottorum non de lapide sed de robore secto totam composuit atque harundine texit)' Bede *Hist. Eccl.* iii. 25. This may be considered the mother-church of the present cathedral at Durham, the chief intermediate links being bishop Eardulph's wooden church at Chester-le-Street (883) and bishop Aldhun's stone church at Durham completed 999, and pulled down to make room for the present structure. On Aug. 11, 1093 the foundation stone of Durham Cathedral was laid in the presence of William of Carileph, bishop of Durham, Turgot, prior of the monastery, afterwards bishop of S. Andrews, and perhaps also Malcolm, king of Scotland. The building went on rapidly, and at the death of William of Carileph

(Jan. 6, 1095—6) was completed from the east end of the choir as far as the first great bay of the nave, including the piers and arches which carry the central tower. Bishop Ralph Flambard (1099—1128) finished the nave, including the side aisles and their roofs as far as the vaultings, and also the western towers up to the height of the nave. See Greenwell *Durham Cathedral* (2nd ed.) p. 21 sq.

20. Ecclesiasticus xlix. 4, 'All, except David and Ezekias and Josias, were defective : for they forsook the law of the most High, even the kings of Juda failed.'

21. The references are 2 Chron. xxxiii. 23, xxxiv. 2, 2 Kings xxi. 13, xxiii. 22, 25.

22. Zechariah xii. 11 'In that day shall there be a great mourning in Jerusalem, as the mourning of Hadadrimmon in the valley of Megiddon.'

23. Revelation xvi. 16.

24. Ecclesiasticus xlix. 1—3.

25. Elfric and Ella were brothers; Osric was the son of Elfric; Edwin and Acha the son and the daughter of Ella; Acha married Ethelfrid and became the mother of Eanfrid, Oswald and Oswy. Oswald was therefore younger brother of Eanfrid, and second cousin (through his mother) of Osric.

The union or separation of the two kingdoms of Bernicia and Deira was bound up with the varying fortunes of the Deiran dynasty of Yffi father of Ella, and the Bernician dynasty of Ida father of Ethelric. Of the Deiran dynasty, Ella, Osric, and Oswin ruled over Deira, and Edwin was strong enough to annex Bernicia also : of the Bernician dynasty, which was the more powerful, Ethelric, Ethelfrid, and Oswald governed Deira as well as Bernicia ; but Oswy until Oswin's death was obliged to be content with Bernicia.

26, 27. Infaustus ille annus et omnibus bonis exosus usque hodie permanet, tam propter apostasiam regum Anglorum qua se fidei sacramentis exuerant, quam propter vesanam Brettonici regis tyrannidem. Unde cunctis placuit regum tempora computantibus, ut ablata de medio regum perfidorum memoria idem annus sequentis regis, id est Osualdi, viri Deo dilecti, regno adsignaretur (This year remains to this day ill-omened and hateful to all good men, both by reason of the apostasy of the kings of the Angles, who had renounced the sacraments of the faith, and because of the mad tyranny of the British king. Wherefore it has seemed good to all who have computed the chronology of the kings to wipe out absolutely the memory of the renegade kings, and to assign the year in question to the reign of the following king, that is Oswald, the man beloved of God) Bede *Hist. Eccl.* iii. 1.

28. Bede *Hist. Eccl.* iii. 2. 'The battle seems to have been fought near S. Oswald's [seven miles north of Hexham]; but Cadwalla fell at a place, on the south and opposite side of the Tyne, called Denisesburna, from the rivulet Denis, now Rowley-water, which flows into the Devil's Water above Dilston.' Greenwell *Durham Cathedral* p. 3.

29. The battle of Maserfield was fought on Aug. 5, 642, eight years after Heavenfield (Bede *Hist. Eccl.* iii. 9). S. Oswald had reconquered Lindsey from Penda, hence his quarrel with the Mercian king. After his victory, Penda struck off S. Oswald's head (as he had struck off Edwin's head nine years before at Hatfield), and set it up on a pole on the battle-field. It was rescued, carried to Lindisfarne, and buried by S. Aidan; but afterwards exhumed and taken to Bamborough, where it remained till S. Cuthbert's time. In 875 when the monks of Lindisfarne retired before the Danes, it was placed in S. Cuthbert's coffin, and accompanied the wanderings of that saint. The historian of the translation of S. Cuthbert's remains in 1104 states that the head was found and left with them (so also Reginald of Durham c. 42, and Malmesb. *Gest. Pontif.* iii. 134). In 1827 when S. Cuthbert's grave was opened the skull was still there (Raine *S. Cuthbert* p. 187). S. Oswald's body was removed by his niece Osthryd to the monastery of Bardney (Bede *Hist. Eccl.* iii. 11), and in the tenth century taken to Gloucester and placed in a shrine.

30. Adamnan *Vita Columbae* i. 1. Oswald told the dream to the abbot Seghine.

31. Plato *Republic* v. 473 (Davies and Vaughan's translation p. 186).

32. Collect in the Sarum use for August 5.

'Omnipotens sempiterne Deus, qui hujus diei jocundam sanctamque laetitiam in sancti servi tui Oswaldi passione consecrasti; da cordibus nostris tui timoris caritatisque augmentum, ut cujus in terris sancti sanguinis effusionem celebramus, illius in caelo collata patrocinia sentiamus. Per Dominum nostrum.' Procter and Wordsworth *Breviarium ad Usum Sarum.* Fasc. iii. p. 589.

33. Bede *Hist. Eccl.* ii. 20.

34. Cadwalla, king of Gwynedd or North Wales, defeated by Edwin 'in his thirst for vengeance allied himself, Briton and Christian as he was, with a Saxon prince who combined in his own person the fiercest energy of a Teuton warrior with the sternest resistance to the progress of the new creed: who, succeeding to power at fifty years old, was for thirty years the prop and the sword of Heathenism, and also came near to reducing the various kingdoms to a monarchy centred in the youngest of them all. This was Penda the Strenuous, king of the Mercians, whose name was long a terror to the inmates of cell and minster in every Christianised district. There is a sort of weird grandeur in the career of one who in his time slew five kings, and might seem as irresistible as destiny.' Bright *Early English Church History* p. 132.

He slew Edwin at Hatfield (633), Egric and Sigebert, kings of East-Anglia (635), Oswald at Maserfield (642), Anna, king of East-Anglia (654), and was himself slain by Oswy at Winwidfield (Nov. 15, 655). 'With Penda fell paganism.' Penda's son, Peada, had been baptized by Finan, bishop of Lindisfarne, two years before his father's death, and when the great kingdom of Mercia became free and united again under Penda's son Wulfhere, the teaching of the Celtic bishops Diuma and Cellach had won its way, and monarch and people embraced Christianity.

35. Bede *Hist. Eccl.* ii. 16.

36. Bede *Hist. Eccl.* iii. 5. The name of the first missionary sent was Corman (Bellenden's *Boece* ix. 20, vol. ii. p. 105).

37. The chief passages in Bede in praise of S. Aidan are *Hist. Eccl.* iii. 3, 5, 14, 17.

38. 'Quid loqueris, rex? Numquid tibi carior est ille filius equae, quam ille filius Dei?' Bede *Hist. Eccl.* iii. 14. 'It seems probable from the gender of this word [equae] that the tradition which represents the bishop as playing in his answer on the words 'mare' and 'Mary' gives the correct version of the story, the former portion of which play on words is given in the Saxon 'myran sunu.' See Higden *Polychronicon* v. 15.' Mayor and Lumby *Bede* p. 247.

39. Cedd (Cedda) was one of four Celtic missionaries sent (653) by Oswy into Mid-Anglia (the part of Mercia which lay between the Trent and the Bedford district) at the request of his son-in-law, the convert Peada,—the first mission to the Midlands. The missionaries also preached in Mercia proper. Cedd however did not remain there many months, being summoned by Oswy to head a mission to the East Saxons, where king Sigebert, who had been baptized by Finan the same year as Peada, was asking for Christian teachers. The next year,—being thirty-eight years after the failure of the Roman mission there by the expulsion of Mellitus from London,—Cedd was consecrated by Finan to be bishop of the East Saxons, but his seat was Tilbury, not London. Bishop Cedd paid many visits to Northumbria and founded

Lastingham. He acted as interpreter at the Council of Whitby (664), and dying of the plague the same year was buried at Lastingham (Bede *Hist. Eccl.* iii. 21—23).

Chad (Ceadda), the younger and more famous brother of Cedd, became abbot of Lastingham on the death of his brother in 664. On the retirement of bishop Colman from Northumbria, Wilfrid had been raised to the see of York, and had gone to France for consecration, but showed no disposition to return; whereupon Oswy prevailed on Chad to become bishop of York, and sent him to Canterbury to be consecrated by archbishop Deusdedit. He found the archbishop dead of the plague, but was consecrated by Wini, bishop of Wessex, and two British bishops. Ceadda continued to act as bishop of York until archbishop Theodore's visitation in 669, who detected the irregularity of his consecration. Chad resigned his see, and retired to Lastingham; but Theodore, who was struck with his piety and humility, on the death of Jaruman, bishop of Mercia, suggested him through Oswy to Wulfhere for the see of Mercia. He had previously corrected the informality of his consecration. Chad's see comprised the whole of Mercia proper, Mid-Anglia, and Lindsey; and his seat was Lichfield. After an exemplary episcopate he died March 2, 672. Bede is loud in his praises of Chad's character (Bede *Hist. Eccl.* iii. 23, 28; iv. 2, 3). Chad is the patron saint of Lichfield.

40. Bede *Hist. Eccl.* iii. 17.

41. S. Aidan's Herrington, and S. Aidan's Benwell in Newcastle-on-Tyne. There are now (April, 1890) in the present diocese of Durham six churches associated with S. Aidan's name; three (at Herrington, Blackhill and South Shields) already consecrated; three (at West Hartlepool, Sunderland and Gateshead) in course of erection, or shortly to be commenced.

42. Coleridge's *Confessions of an Inquiring Mind* p. 307 (*ed.* Bohn).

43. The exact date of S. Hilda's death is November 17, 680 (anno Dominicae incarnationis sexcentesimo octogesimo die quintadecima kalendarum Decembrium Bede *Hist. Eccl.* iv. 23). Her day has been misplaced, and is usually, but wrongly, kept on November 18 (Alban Butler).

44. Hild is the name of a Saxon war-goddess; Hilda is the Scandinavian goddess of war and victory; Veleda, a German deified heroine, is mentioned in Tacitus *Germ.* 8; *Hist.* iv. 61, 65; Statius *Silv.* 1. iv. 90.

45. The site of S. Hilda's monastery on the Wear has not been identified. Bede describes it as a small establishment, locum unius familiae ad septentrionalem plagam Viuri fluminis (a piece of land of one family on the north side of the river Wear) *Hist. Eccl.* iv. 23. Hilda left it after a year (? 649) to succeed Heiu as abbess of Hartlepool (Hereteu). Here she remained eight years. She was then thirteen years (657—680) at Whitby.

On the Church of S. Hilda at South Shields, Hutchinson (*History of Durham* ii. p. 606) writes: 'The antiquity of the church at Shields is not to be deduced with accuracy from any records before us; it was perhaps nearly cotemporary with that of Jarrow.'

46. These pupils were Bosa and Wilfrid II, bishops of York, Ætla, bishop of Dorchester, Oftfor, bishop of Worcester and S. John of Beverley, bishop of Hexham, afterwards translated to York.

47. Monile pretiosissimum, quod dum attentius consideraret tanti fulgore luminis refulgere videbatur, ut omnes Britanniae fines illius gratia splendoris impleret. Bede *Hist. Eccl.* iv. 23.

48. Isaiah xl. 6, 8.

49. 'The Lindisfarne Gospels was written by Eadfrith in honour of God and S. Cuthbert and all the saints in the island. Eadfrith ruled as bishop over the Lindisfarnensian Church from 698 to 721, but the book was probably written before he became bishop. The ornamentation was the work of Ethelwold, who was bishop from 724 to 740. Bilfrith, the anchorite, added the jewelled binding. The interlinear English gloss was made by Aldred, the priest, about the middle of the tenth century. The several facts are recorded in an entry at the end of the book, in the handwriting of Aldred.' Greenwell *Durham Cathedral* (ed. 2), p. 6. This book is now preserved in the British Museum (MS. Cotton, Nero, D. iv). 'It is still marked with the stain caused by the sea-water.' Raine *Cuthbert* in Smith's Dictionary of Christian Biography.

50. Bede *Vita Cuthberti* c. 37 sq. (iv. p. 323 sq. *ed.* Giles).

51. In 793 the monastery of Lindisfarne was surprised and ravaged by a marauding party of Danes, but S. Cuthbert's body was untouched. In 875 on the approach of Halfden, a Danish chieftain of exceptional ferocity, Eardulph bishop of Lindisfarne, with Eadred the abbot and most of the monks, took the coffin containing S. Cuthbert's body and S. Oswald's head, the Lindisfarne Gospels, Ethelwold's stone crucifix and other treasures, and abandoned the island which for two hundred and forty years had been associated with the evangelisation of England. Their first intention to sail to Ireland having been frustrated in the manner already described, they wandered from one place of retreat to another for nearly seven years, till they settled at Craik, near York, where they remained four months. Here, according to Symeon of Durham our chief authority, S. Cuthbert in a vision to Eadred commanded the Danes and Angles to ransom a certain slave named Guthred of noble Danish birth, and to make him king of Northumbria. Alfred acknowledged the new king, and peace being now restored, bishop and abbot moved the sacred remains from Craik to Chester-le-Street (883), where Eardulph built a church of wood. Guthred in pious gratitude gave to the church of S. Cuthbert all the land between the Tyne and the Wear (Simeon says, between the Tyne and the Tees, inter duo flumina Tinam et Teisam), which from that time formed the main part of the 'Patrimony of S. Cuthbert.' At Chester-le-Street nine bishops ruled in peaceful succession till 990, when on the threat of another Danish invasion bishop Aldhun following the earlier precedent removed the body once more, this time to Ripon. But the storm passed over speedily: the exiles set off for their old home at Chester-le-Street, and were within six miles of it, when the halt at Dunholme brought to a close the romantic history of their wanderings, and fixed the final restingplace of the saint at Durham. Once only subsequently, in 1069, when, in revenge for the death of Cumin, William the Conqueror was harrying all the land north of York, S. Cuthbert's body was taken to its old home in Lindisfarne; but after three months was brought safely back to Durham again.

52. The eider duck (anas mollissima), called S. Cuthbert's duck, 'found on the Fern Isles on the Northumberland coast, which is the only place where they are known to breed in England,' Bewick *History of Birds* ii. p. 318 (*ed.* 1, Newcastle 1804). When the saint's tomb was opened in 1827, figures of these birds were found worked in cloth of gold on the episcopal vestments which wrapped his body. See the illustrations in Raines' *Saint Cuthbert* 1828.

53. Bede *Vita S. Cuthberti* xii. Compare the story told in c. x. of the two 'quadrupeds called otters' (quadrupedia, quae vulgo lutrae vocantur), and their devotion to the saint.

54. Dum passionis Dominicae mysteria celebraret, imitaretur ipse quod ageret seipsum videlicet Deo in cordis contritione mactando. Bede *Vita S. Cuthberti* xvi.

55. Cuthbert, a monk of Jarrow, in a letter to Cuthwin, a fellow-student.

56. Cuthbert's letter is given in full in Giles' edition of Bede's Works 1 p. clxiii., and in Mayor and Lumby *Bede* p. 176 sq.

57. The Revised Version of the New Testament was published on May 17, 1881, six weeks before this sermon was preached.

58. See Westcott *History of the English Bible* p. 105 sq. (*ed.* 1).

59. Richard de Bury was the son of Sir Richard Aungervile, and was born 24 January 1287 (or 1281) near Bury St Edmunds, from which place he takes his name. After a distinguished career at Oxford he was appointed governor of Prince Edward of Windsor, afterwards Edward III., who, on his accession in 1327, showed the gratitude of a devoted pupil by loading him with honours. In 1330 and 1333 he was sent as ambassador to the Papal Court at Avignon, and on the former of these visits made the acquaintance of Petrarch, who refers to him more than once. Throughout these diplomatic missions De Bury maintained a dignity and splendour in keeping with the spirit of the age which was an age of display. In 1333 he added to his existing appointments those of chaplain of the papal chapel and dean of Wells. On the death of Louis de Beaumont, bishop of Durham (25 Sept. 1333), the Prior and Convent elected their subprior Robert de Graystanes, who was consecrated by the archbishop of York, and duly installed at Durham. But the interest of the king and the pope in De Bury's favour was too strong to be resisted, and Graystanes returned to his convent 'a bishop without a bishopric.' On 5 June 1334 De Bury was enthroned at Durham with great magnificence in the presence of the king and queen, the queen mother, the king of the Scots and the two archbishops. The same year saw him nominated Lord Treasurer, which office he resigned a few months later on his appointment as Lord Chancellor. But war with France was imminent, and his services were necessary for delicate diplomatic negociations both at home and abroad. In 1338 he accompanied king Edward in his stately progress up the Rhine to his meeting with the emperor Lewis at Coblentz. What with frequent missions on the continent, with threatened attacks from the Scotch (which as prince palatine he had to meet) and with his episcopal duties, De Bury must have been fully occupied during these years; and yet all this time we find him in constant correspondence with literary men, gathering scholars around him, employing at Auckland a staff of copyists and illuminators, enlisting in his behalf the services of monks and travellers to rescue and to purchase rare volumes, and collecting a library such that, as was commonly said, he had more books than all the other bishops in England. After 1341, when he ceased to go abroad, he devoted himself more and more to the literary pursuits which he loved so well, and finished his *Philobiblon* on his birthday, 24 January 1345, dying at Auckland on 14 April of the same year. Though forced by the exigencies of the age and by his own capacity for public affairs to be a diplomatist and a statesman, he was essentially a lover of peace and of books. The *Querimonia Librorum contra Bella* in his *Philobiblon* shows us this. He was both a scholar and a patron of scholars. His choice library he destined for a college which it was his intention to found at Oxford, and he gave elaborate directions for the keeping of the books; but it is doubtful whether either design was fully carried out. His great hospitality and his charities, which were organized on a vast scale, left him very poor, and we have evidence that his executors were obliged to sell many of his books to pay his debts. It was left to his successor bishop Hatfield to found Durham College at Oxford. If his library went, as is traditionally stated, to the Durham Benedictines at Oxford, it was dispersed on the dissolution of the college by Henry VIII. For his life see William de Chambre in Wharton's *Anglia Sacra* I. 765, *Historiae Dunelmensis Scriptores* (Surtees Society Publications 1839), Creighton *Richard De Bury* in the Dictionary of National Biography, and E. C. Thomas *The Philobiblon of Richard de Bury* (1888).

60. *Philobiblon* prol. (pp. 1, 3 sq, 155, 156 sq, *ed.* Thomas).

61. Rev. Charles Thomas Whitley, Hon. D.D. of Durham University, Honorary Canon of Durham Cathedral and Vicar of Bedlington, who was nominated Proctor with Rev. Thomas Williamson Peile M.A. at the first meeting of Convocation held on March 4, 1836.

Rev. John Cundill, Hon. D.D. of Durham University, Honorary Canon of Durham Cathedral, and from 1842 to 1889 Rector of S. Margaret's Durham, who appears as a student of the foundation with eighteen others (in the first Durham University Calendar, 1833, pp. 12, 13).

These two were present at the Jubilee Festival, and are doubtless alluded to here.

[I am indebted for these facts to Rev. J. T. Fowler M.A., Librarian of Durham University.]

62. William the Conqueror built the Castle of Durham (c. 1072) as a protection to the bishop; Hugh Pudsey (bishop, 1153—1194) restored some part of the building which had suffered from fire, built the gallery with its wonderful Norman door and erected the original hall, which was a magnificent structure, 'one hundred and twenty yards in length, of a proportionable height and width, and lighted on every side.' This prelate likewise built at the west end of the Cathedral the famous Galilee chapel, which was originally designed for a lady-chapel at the eastern extremity. Thomas de Hatfield (bishop, 1345—1381) strengthened the tower of the castle, and built the constable's hall and the present banqueting hall, which last Richard Fox (bishop, 1494—1501), the founder of Corpus Christi College, Oxford, found too large for his purpose and reduced by one-third of its length by cutting off the present kitchen. See Hutchinson *History of Durham* ii. 358 sq.

63. Like the body of S. Cuthbert, the relics of the venerable Bede have had a chequered history. Originally laid to rest in Jarrow, they were stolen between 1031 and 1041 by an enthusiastic monk Elfred, brought to Durham, and placed in the coffin of S. Cuthbert. Pudsey removed them to a golden shrine on the right side of the body of the saint. In 1370 they were moved into the Galilee by Richard de Castro Bernardi (Greenwell *Durham Cathedral* p. 43; Giles in his edition of Bede's Works, 1. p. xliii, makes Pudsey move them into the Galilee). They lie on the south side of Galilee, with a plain slab over them, on which in 1830 was carved the well-known inscription Hac sunt in fossa Bedae venerabilis ossa. For the medieval story in connexion with this inscription see the authorities given in Giles p. ciii sq.

64. Benedict Biscop, a Saxon of noble birth, who held office under Oswy, and had been endowed by him with an estate suitable to his dignity, at twenty-five 'renounced the secular life, despising the service of this world that he might enlist in the ranks of the true King.' Accompanied by Wilfrid, his junior by a few years, he started for Rome in 653, left Wilfrid behind at Lyons, and worshipped at the tombs of the Apostles. He returned home full of love and veneration for what he had seen. Smitten with his enthusiasm Alchfrid, Oswy's son, would have accompanied him on a second journey, but his father could not spare him; and in 665 Benedict went to Rome alone. He now retired to the monastery of Lerins to study the monastic system, of which he was enamoured. Here he received the tonsure and remained two years, till summoned by pope Vitalian to accompany to Canterbury the newly-consecrated archbishop Theodore, and to assist him with his knowledge of England and the English tongue. After two years in Kent he took a third journey to Rome and returned with many books of sacred learning. Egfrid was now king of Northumbria. To his court Benedict came, and displayed the holy volumes and relics which he had brought; whereupon the king at once made him a grant of land on the north side of the Wear, on which to build a monastery (674). Benedict, without loss of time, repaired to France to find masons, and such was their diligence that within a year the monastery of Wearmouth was nearly completed. He next sent to France for workers in glass, from whom the English learnt the art of glazing windows and making vessels of glass. Two years before, Wilfrid had introduced the first glass windows into England at York and Ripon. Vessels for the altar and vestments, which could not be had in Britain, Benedict procured from abroad. What could not be obtained from Gaul must be fetched from Rome, so thither he went for the fourth time and returned with great store of books, bringing with him John, precentor of S. Peter's and abbot of S. Martin's at Rome, to teach the English Gregorian music. He brought back also, at king Egfrid's instance, letters of privilege for his monastery from Pope Agatho, and pictures of sacred subjects to teach the common people through the eye what they could not learn from books. So pleased was the king, that he made Benedict another grant of land at the mouth of the Tyne to build a second monastery. This was Jarrow. Twenty-two brethren, with Ceolfrid as abbot, were told off to form the new society (682). But the new monastery must be furnished as completely as the old, so, leaving Easterwin in charge of Wearmouth, Biscop went a fifth time to Rome in search of sacred books and manuscripts. Much sorrow awaited him on his return. His patron Egfrid had been slain in battle, and the pestilence had been busy at both his monasteries. At Wearmouth, Easterwin had been struck down at thirty-six; at Jarrow, all who were able to chant the service had been taken away, save Ceolfrid and one little boy, who struggled on, as best they might, to perform the daily offices, only for a time (and it cost them many tears to have to make the omission) foregoing the antiphons at matins and vespers. And now Biscop's active career was drawing to a close. He was smitten with paralysis, and for three years lay in entire helplessness, cheerful and studious, through sleepless nights and weary days, while Ceolfrid ruled both monasteries, for Sigfrid, Easterwin's successor, was slowly dying of consumption. Most touching is Bede's account of the two sufferers; how when the end drew near, as neither could move, Sigfrid was brought in his couch into Benedict's cell, laid on the same bed and their heads brought together that they might kiss each other. Benedict survived Sigfrid four months, and died Jan. 14, 690. See Bede *Vitae Beatorum Abbatum*, and Low *Diocesan History of Durham* p. 65 sq., from which the foregoing account is abridged.

65. The date of Bede's death (735) was probably the date of Alcuin's birth. A Northumbrian of the noble house from which had sprung S. Willibrord, the Apostle of the Frisians, he was brought up from infancy in Egbert's school at York, of which he was himself afterwards the chief exponent and the brightest glory. In the zenith of his intellectual vigour as a teacher he was sent to Rome in 780 by archbishop Eanbald to bring back his pall, and falling in with Charles the Great, who had previously shown him distinguished marks of favour, was induced by him to join his court, and to take charge of the Palatine schools. At Troyes, Ferrières, and afterwards at Tours were his chief colleges, and thither flocked all the famous men of his age to sit at his feet. He only paid one short visit to England (790—2) and died at Tours. Of his indebtedness to Bede the present Bishop of Oxford writes (*Alcuin* in Smith's Dictionary of Christian Biography) 'The schools of Northumbria had gathered in the harvest of Irish learning, of the Franco-Gallican schools still subsisting and preserving a remnant of classical character in the sixth century, and of Rome, itself now barbarized. Bede had received instruction from the disciples of Chad and Cuthbert in the Irish studies on the scriptures, from Wilfrid and Acca in the French and Roman learning, and from Benedict Biscop and Albinus in the combined and organized discipline of Theodore. By his influence with Egbert, the school of York was founded; in it was centred nearly all the wisdom of the West, and its greatest pupil was Alcuin. Whilst learning had been growing in Northumbria, it had been declining on the continent: in the latter days of Alcuin the decline of English learning began..., at the same time the continent was gaining peace and organization under Charles. Alcuin carried the learning which would have perished in England, into France and Germany.'

66. William of Durham in 1248 bequeathed money to found University College Oxford. He died at Rouen in 1249, and is usually identified with William de Laneham, who was archdeacon of Durham and rector of Bishopwearmouth. The scheme however was not carried out for some few years (Maxwell Lyte *History of the University of Oxford* p. 70 sq). Hugh of Balsham, bishop of Ely, founded S. Peter's College Cambridge in 1257. Walter of Merton, bishop of Rochester, founded Merton College Oxford in 1274.

67. William Van Mildert (bishop, 1826—1836).

68. Vir ardentis ingenii nec literarum inscius, abditarum rerum ab adolescentia super fidem curiosus (A man of fervid genius with a considerable knowledge of literature, from his youth up devoted in an astonishing way to the study of abstruse subjects). Petrarch *De Reb. Fam.* iii. 1.

69. *Philobiblon* xix. (pp. 141 sq., 245 sq. *ed.* Thomas).

70. The petition was made in 1650, but the letters patent for the erection of the college were not issued until 1657. See Low *Durham Diocesan History* p. 265 sq.

71. The Durham mitre is encircled by a prince's coronet; the bishop of Durham crosses the sword and the crozier; in his official acts he declares himself to be bishop 'by divine providence' instead of 'by divine permission'; with the bishops of London and Winchester he takes his seat in the House of Lords at once by right of his see, without waiting for his turn in seniority, and at coronations he supports the sovereign on the right hand. These are, I believe, the only vestiges now remaining of the Palatinate power. On the rights of the Prince Palatine in the olden time see Low *Durham Diocesan History* p. 122 sq.

72. William Van Mildert, the learned editor of Waterland's works, was translated from Llandaff to Durham in 1826, and held the bishopric ten years. The Reform Bill of 1832 was soon followed by the appointment of the Ecclesiastical Commissioners, who were incorporated in 1836. The income of the bishop was reduced to eight thousand a year, and of the twelve canonries six were abolished. The Palatinate was to be annexed to the Crown on the next avoidance of the See. But the establishment of Durham University preceded the recommendations of the Commission, and came as a graceful and spontaneous act from the Bishop and the Dean and Chapter. The revenues of the Cathedral furnished the endowment, and the Bishop gave up his Castle at Durham for the use of the students of the new foundation. Van Mildert died Feb. 21, 1836, and, as the last Prince Palatine, was honoured with a resting place in the Chapel of the Nine Altars near S. Cuthbert's shrine.

73. Ecclesiasticus xliv. 4.

74. *Fundamenta ejus super montibus sanctis* ('Her foundations are upon the holy hills,' Prayer-Book Version) Ps. lxxxvii. 1, corresponding to Ps. lxxxvi. 1 in the Vulgate, is the motto of Durham University.

75. Ecclesiasticus xliv. 2.

76. On the pedestal of the chalice were engraved the following lines:—

Hic ciphus insignis fit Presulis ex tetra signis
Ri : Dunolmensis quarti natu Byriensis,
given in Raine *Auckland Castle* p. 36 from Chambre.

77. Bernard Gilpin, the 'Apostle of the North,' was born at Kentmere in Westmoreland in 1517. At the age of sixteen he went to Queen's College Oxford, where he distinguished himself in Greek and Hebrew, was elected a Fellow, and was one of the first of the brilliant band of scholars invited to join Wolsey's new foundation at Christ Church. At this time Gilpin was still a staunch supporter of the unreformed religion, and as such held a public conference at Oxford with John Hooper, and afterwards (May, 1549) with Peter Martyr, then divinity professor, who speaks highly of his temperate conduct during the disputation. But already a change was working in his mind; he determined to search out the truth for himself by a diligent study of the fathers, and consulted Tonstall, bishop of Durham, his mother's uncle, on transubstantiation and other points. He was now appointed vicar of Norton in Durham, and, as was customary in the case of crown appointments, preached before the court at Greenwich, when instead of the usual laudatory sermon he launched out against the abuses of patrons, pluralists, and non-residents. His theological views continuing unsettled, he now, at Tonstall's suggestion and expense, travelled abroad; and, much to the bishop's concern, first resigned Norton. 'You might still hold it with a dispensation.' 'In my absence the Devil will not be held by any dispensation.' After three years spent at Mechlin, Louvain and Paris, where he printed Tonstall's book on the Eucharist, he returned to England, though Mary was on the throne, and he himself more Protestant than before. Made archdeacon of Durham and rector of Easington, his zeal for reform in morals and religion raised him up many enemies. These accused him to Tonstall, who said, 'Father's soul, let him alone: he hath more learning than you all:' and on his resigning his rectory with his archdeaconry appointed him rector of Houghton-le-Spring and wished to force a canonry upon him. His enemies now brought thirty-two counts against him before Bonnor, bishop of London, who, acting under the Queen's commission, sent a pursuivant to bring him to London. On the way Gilpin accidentally broke his leg, which probably saved his life, as, before he reached his destination, Mary had died. Elizabeth on the throne, he was offered the bishopric of Carlisle and the provostship of Queen's College; but refused both. He now devoted himself heart and soul to his parochial work at Houghton. Not content with evangelizing his own parish he used the general licence to preach, which he possessed, to pay yearly missionary visits to the most neglected parts of Northumberland, Yorkshire, Westmoreland and Cumberland. Redesdale and Tynedale, considered the most barbarous districts in the North, were favourite scenes of his preaching tours. Here his influence was unbounded. The incident of the fray in Rothbury Church is given below. The story of his taking down a glove, which hung as a challenge in a churchyard, is also well known. A thief who had unwittingly stolen his horses brought them back in terror when he learnt whose they were. His charity and his sympathy were wonderful. He would sometimes strip off his cloak, and give it to an ill-clad beggar. Riding with his servants in the country he saw a poor farmer's horse fall down dead in the plough. Immediately Gilpin told one of his servants to unsaddle his horse, and give it to the man. Though not exceptionally wealthy, yet by careful economy he was able to exercise great hospitality. His custom was on Sundays to feast all his parishioners in three divisions according to their rank. An unexpected visit by Lord Burleigh found him able to entertain his retinue in such a style that 'they could not have expected more at Lambeth.' He met the ignorance of his time by constantly having poor scholars round him, by educating five or six young men continually at the universities at his own expense, and by founding the famous Kepier Grammar school at Houghton. Such fame and influence as his raised up detractors. He was accused not now of Protestantism but of Romanism; and called upon to preach at a minute's notice before bishop Barnes at Chester-le-Street. His sermon was a plain and bold exposure of the lamentable state of the diocese. The sermon over, the bishop said: 'Father Gilpin, I acknowledge you are fitter to be bishop of Durham, than myself parson of this church of yours. I ask forgiveness for errors: forgive me, father. I know you have hatched up some chickens that now seek to pick out your eyes; but so long as I shall live bishop of Durham, be secure. No man shall injure you.' Gilpin died March 4, 1583, in his sixty-sixth year. See his life by Carleton, bishop of Chichester, in Wordsworth's *Ecclesiastical Biography*, iv. p. 85 sq., Perry in *Dictionary of National Biography*, and Collingwood *Memoirs of Bernard Gilpin*.

78. Norton and Easington.

79. Called by Gilpin the Kepier Grammar-School, from the fact that the revenues were in part derived from the tithes (hence called Gilley tithes) of the dissolved hospital of S. Giles at Kepier near Durham, the seat of the Heaths. John Heath of Kepier is mentioned in the charter of Gilpin's School. Hutchinson *History of Durham* ii. p. 709.

80. At Rothbury, two factions, who 'practised a bloody manner of revenge, termed by them Deadly-feod,' when Gilpin was in the pulpit came to church and stood, the one of them in the chancel, the other in the body of the church, armed with swords and javelins. 'Mr Gilpin, somewhat mooved with this unaccustomed spectacle, goeth on neverthelesse in his sermon, and now a second time their weapons make a clashing sound, and the one side drew neerer to the other, so that they were in danger to fall to blowes in the middest of the church. Hereupon Mr Gilpin commeth downe from the pulpit, and stepping to the ringleaders of either faction, first of all he appeased the tumult. Next, he labowreth to establishe peace betwixt them, but he could not prevaile in that: onely they promised to keepe the peace unbroken so long as Mr Gilpin should remaine in the church. Mr Gilpin, seeing he could not utterly extinguish the hatred which was now inveterate betwixt them, desired them that yet they would forbear hostility so long as he should remaine in those quarters: and this they consented unto. Mr Gilpin thereupon goeth up into the pulpit againe (for he had not made an end of his sermon) and spent the rest of the allotted time in disgracing that barbarous and bloody custome of theirs and (if it were possible) in the utter banishing of it for ever. So often as Mr Gilpin came into those parts afterwardes, if any man amongst them stood in feare of a deadly foe he resorted usually where Mr Gilpin was, supposing himselfe more safe in his company, then if he went with a guard.' Carleton *Life of Gilpin* reprinted in Wordsworth *Ecclesiastical Biography* iv. 116 sq.

81. The first quotation is from Peter Martyr's account of his disputation with Gilpin in 1549 (Carleton *Life of Gilpin* p. 89); the second from Edward Irving's preface to Gilpin's Life given in Collingwood *Memoirs of Bernard Gilpin* p. 285.

82. William Gilpin *Life of Bernard Gilpin* p. 127 (Cox, 1854).

83. The chief dates in Cosin's life are as follows: 1596, born at Norwich; 1610, to Caius College Cambridge; 1616, librarian to bishop Overall; 1619, in the house of bishop Neile; 1625, married, made archdeacon of the East Riding and rector of Elwick; 1627, publishes his Book of Private Devotions; 1634, master of Peterhouse; 1643, dean of Peterborough; 1641, impeached in the House of Commons and deprived of his preferments; 1642—1659, in France living in great poverty; 1660, made bishop of Durham; 1672, died in

London Jan. 15, and buried in the chapel at Auckland Castle April 29.

84. Richard Poor (bishop of Durham, 1228—1237) has been suggested with great probability as the builder of the hall. We know that he was an enthusiastic architect, for, before his translation to Durham, when bishop of Salisbury he had commenced the cathedral there. That the present chapel was originally intended for a banqueting hall is proved, among other evidence, by the discovery about five years ago of the heads of three doors in its east wall. The two chapels, situated one above the other, which existed in Tonstall's time, were blown up by Sir Arthur Hazelrig, who purchased Auckland Castle during the Commonwealth. They formed the wing on the south side of the building, parallel to the present chapel; and the foundations of this wing can still be traced beneath the turf.

85. Thomas Morton was a man of great learning, and distinguished for humility and benevolence. When parish priest at Long Marston, near York, his conduct during the plague had been most devoted and heroic. He was made bishop of Chester in 1616, translated to Lichfield in 1618, and to Durham in 1631. Kindliness, liberality and conscientiousness characterised his episcopal administration. He twice entertained king Charles at Durham. In 1641 he was committed to the Tower with other bishops; in 1646 episcopacy was abolished, and the bishop's estates sold. But bishop Morton's high character was such that he was treated leniently at first, until for baptizing a daughter of the Earl of Rutland he was committed to prison for six months. Released he wandered about, till meeting Sir C. Yelverton, a parliamentary leader, he was invited to become tutor to his son. Here he lived happily and died Sep. 22, 1659, a few months before the Restoration, in his ninety-fifth year.

86. 'George Davenport succeeded Sancroft at Houghton-le-Spring, but like a worthy successor of Bernard Gilpin, he refused to accept any additional preferment, saying that he "had more preferment, and a better worldly estate than he could show good husbandry, and he feared to die with any of the Church's goods in his hands." Besides rebuilding his rectory, to which he added a chapel, he built and endowed one half of the almshouse at Houghton. He died in 1677, much lamented by his flock. He was the keeper of Bishop Cosin's library at Durham, which is indebted to him for many very valuable manuscripts.' Low *Diocesan History of Durham*, p. 288, and *Surtees Society* vol. xxxvii p. 17.

87. 'June 29, 1665. By water to Whitehall, where the **court full of waggons and people ready to go out of town**. This end of the town every day growing very bad of the plague. The Mortality Bill is come to 267; which is about ninety more than the last; and of these but four in the City, which is a great blessing to us.' Pepys' Diary.

88. Five metropolitans and fifty-two **other bishops from the United States** of America, the **Dominion of Canada, India,** and the **Colonies were** present at the **reopening of the** chapel. Their names are recorded on two brass tablets placed in the antechapel, and in the prayer books which, as a memorial of **their visit, they presented to** Bishop Lightfoot for the use of the chapel.

The inscription **in the antechapel runs as** follows:—

HOC . SACELLVM

EX . VETVSTA . DOMVS . AVLA . REFECTVM

CONSECRAVIT

JOHANNES . COSINVS . EPISC .

IN . FESTO . S . PETRI . A . D . MDCLXV .

REDINTEGRATVM . ET . ADORNATVM

ITERVM . DEDICAVIT

JOSEPHVS . B . LIGHTFOOT . EPISC .

ENCAENIA . CELEBRATA . SVNT . KAL . AVGVSTIS

A . D . MDCCCLXXXVIII .

ADSISTENTIBVS EPISCOPIS

ASIAE . AFRICAE . AMERICAE . AVSTRALIAE .

INSVLARVM . OCEANI .

———

QVID . RETRIBVAM . DOMINO ?

89. Among those who refused to take the oath of allegiance **to** William and Mary were archbishop Sancroft, bishops Ken, Turner, Frampton, Lloyd, White, Thomas, Lake, and Cartwright, and about four hundred clergy. These were all deprived. Among the more **remarkable** of the divines who refused the oath were John Kettlewell **and George** Hickes, Jeremy Collier, the Church historian, and Charles **Leslie, and** among laymen Henry Dodwell, Camden Professor at **Oxford,** and Robert Nelson. **In** the diocese of Durham, Denys Granville, son-in-law of bishop Cosin, dean and archdeacon of Durham, became a non-juror, went into exile, **and died in great** poverty.

90. See the *Guardian* for July 11, 1888, p. 1031.

91. Fuller *Church History of Britain* vi. p. 440 (*ed.* Brewer).

92. See Evelyn's Diary '1 Oct. 1651. The Dean [Dr Cosin] dining this day at our house, told me the occasion of publishing those Offices which among the Puritans were wont to be call'd *Cosins cousining Devotions* by way of derision. At the first coming of the Queene into England, she and her French ladys were often upbraiding our religion, that had neither appointed nor set forth any houres of prayer or breviaries, by which ladys and courtiers, who have much spare time, might edify and be in devotion, as they had. Our Protestant ladys, scandaliz'd it seemes at this, mov'd the matter to the King, whereupon his Majesty presently call'd Bishop White to him...On which the Bishop told his Majesty that it might be don easily and was very necessary; whereupon the King commanded him to employ some person of the Cleargy to compile such a work, and presently the Bishop naming Dr Cosin, the King injoyn'd him to charge the doctor in his name to set about it immediately...This I mention to justify that industrious and pious Deane, who had exceedingly suffer'd by it, as if he had don it of his owne head to introduce Popery, from which no man was more averse, and one who in this time of temptation and apostacy held and confirm'd many to our Church.'

93. The Savoy Conference for the Revision of the Prayer Book held in the lodgings of the bishop of London at the Savoy in the Strand 1661. Richard Baxter, the most prominent on the presbyterian side, has left us an account of it in his *History of his Life and Times*, from vol. I. p. 172 of which work (*ed.* Calamy) the quotation in question is taken.

94. The quotation is from a private letter from James Sharp (then a presbyterian, afterwards archbishop of St Andrews) to Robert Douglass, a minister at Edinburgh, dated May 29, 1660, given in *A True and Impartial Account of the Life of Dr James Sharp* (1723) p. 104.

95. Wakeman *The Church and the Puritans* in Epochs of Church History p. 184.

96. Fuller *Church History of Britain* I. p. lix. (*ed.* Brewer).

97. Johnson *Lives of the Poets* i. p. 245 (Parker 1864).

98. Bartlett *Memoirs of Bishop Butler* p. 96.

99. The reference is to the windows on the north and south walls, the work of Messrs Burlison and Grylls under Bishop Lightfoot's direction. The following is an extract from the bishop's description of them.

'The series proceeds from right to left, beginning with the easternmost window on the north wall and ending with the easternmost window on the south wall. For purposes of description each window may be divided into three portions; (i) *Angels with Scrolls*. These occupy the central lower compartment. The scrolls bear the names of the earlier occupants of the Northumbrian See. This was placed at Lindisfarne by Aidan A.D. 635 and remained there till Eardulph A.D. 875. Meanwhile an offshoot was planted at Hexham (Hagustald) under whose jurisdiction the county of Durham fell for a time, and this existed from Tunbert (A.D. 681) to Tidferth (A.D. 814). From Lindisfarne the see was removed to Cestria (Chester-le-street) and remained there till A.D. 995, when it was removed by Aldhun to Durham. The names on the six scrolls are those of the bishops of (1) (2) Lindisfarne, (3) (4) Hexham, and (5) Chester, ending with (6) the earlier bishops of Durham. (ii) *Tracery*. This consists mainly of three quatrefoils in the easternmost window on either wall; and of a large cusped circle in the other four windows. All these are filled with figures of the principal personages belonging to the successive periods to which the historical scenes beneath refer. (iii) *Historical Scenes*. Of these there are three in each window, making eighteen in all. The nine on the north wall comprise the *Celtic* period of Northumbrian history ending with the Council of Whitby and the submission to Rome. The nine on the south wall give the *Roman* period to the building of Durham Cathedral.

FIRST WINDOW. (i) *Angel's Scroll*. The earliest bishops of Lindisfarne from Aidan (A.D. 635) to Eadfrid (A.D. 698). (ii) *Tracery*. Three small lights; figures of K. Edwin, of Paulinus and of K. Oswald. (iii) *Historical Scenes*. 1. Paulinus preaching in the Court of Edwin; flight of the dove through the hall (First Conversion of Northumbria). 2. King Oswald planting the Cross before the battle of Heavenfield. 3. S. Aidan leaving the shores of Iona to preach the Gospel in Northumbria (Second Conversion of Northumbria). SECOND WINDOW. (i) *Angel's Scroll*. The succeeding bishops of Lindisfarne from Ethelwold (A.D. 724) to Eardulph (A.D. 854). (ii) *Tracery*. Figure of S. Aidan seated, with the legend PETRA UNDE EXCISI ESTIS (Is. li. 1). (iii) *Historical Scenes*. 4. S. Aidan preaching and king Oswald interpreting. 5. S. Aidan teaching the English youths. 6. S. Finan baptising Peada king of the Mid-Anglians (representing the missionary work of the Northumbrian Church). THIRD WINDOW. (i) *Angel's Scroll*. The first bishops of Hexham from Tunbert (A.D. 681) to

Frethbert (A.D. 734). (ii) *Tracery*. Figure of S. Hilda seated, with the legend SURREXIT MATER IN ISRAEL (Judges v. 7). (iii) *Historical Scenes*. 7. S. Hilda receiving the poet Cædmon into her monastery at Whitby (the beginnings of English literature). 8. S. Hilda is consulted by kings and bishops. 9. The Council of Whitby, at which S. Hilda is present on the Celtic side. FOURTH WINDOW. (i) *Angel's Scroll*. The succeeding bishops of Hexham from Alchmund (A.D. 767) to Tidferth (A.D. 814). (ii) *Tracery*. Figure of S. Cuthbert, with the legend SUSTULIT EUM DE GREGIBUS OVIUM (Ps. lxxviii. 70). (iii) *Historical Scenes*. 10. The youth Cuthbert presents himself to the abbot Boisil and asks admission to Melrose. 11. Consecration of S. Cuthbert by archbishop Theodore. 12. Death of S. Cuthbert, announced by the attendant monks to their brethren at Lindisfarne by lighted torches. FIFTH WINDOW. (i) *Angel's Scroll*. The bishops of Cestria (Chester-le-Street) from Cutheard (A.D. 900) to Aldhun (A.D. 990). (ii) *Tracery*. Figure of the Venerable Bede, with the legend SCRIBA DOCTUS IN REGNO CAELORUM (Matt. xiii. 52). (iii) *Historical Scenes*. 13. The abbot Ceolfrid and the boy Bede singing the antiphons during the plague. 14. The erection of Benedict Biscop's twin monasteries. Wearmouth is represented as already built in the background, and the plan of Jarrow is in Benedict's hands. 15. The death of Bede on completing his translation of S. John's Gospel. SIXTH WINDOW. (i) *Angel's Scroll*. The earliest bishops of Durham from Aldhun (A.D. 995) to William de S. Barbara (A.D. 1143). (ii) *Tracery*. Three small lights, containing the figures of king Alfred, bishop Aldhun, and prior Turgot. (iii) *Historical Scenes*. 16. Discovery of the lost volume of the Gospels during the wanderings of the body of S. Cuthbert from Lindisfarne to Chester-le-Street. 17. King Athelstan presenting his offerings at the shrine of S. Cuthbert at Chester-le-Street. 18. Building of Durham Cathedral by William of Carileph.'

 1. See Bartlett *Memoirs of Bishop Butler* p. 225. The remark was made to Dr Foster, bishop Butler's chaplain.

 2. The words occur in an epitaph from an anonymous correspondent published in the *London Magazine* for May 1754, and in Webb's *Collection of Epitaphs* i. 97. The first four lines are as follow:—

   Beneath this marble Butler lies entombed,
    Who, with a soul inflamed by love divine,
    His life in presence of his God consumed
     Like the bright lamps before the holy shrine.

The whole epitaph is given in Bartlett's *Memoirs* p. 228.

3. Matthew Arnold *Bishop Butler and the Zeit-Geist* in *Last Essays on Church and Religion* (1877) pp. 78, 86.

4. 'We should study what S. James, with wonderful elegance and expressiveness, calls meekness of wisdom in our behaviour towards all men.' Bishop Butler *Charge to the Durham Clergy* 1751.

5. Rev. C. H. Spurgeon in *Feathers for Arrows* p. 204 (Passmore and Alabaster 1870).

6. From 'The Bird, the Chorister and the Angels' in *Songs Old and New* by Mrs Rundle Charles, author of 'Chronicles of the Schönberg-Cotta Family.' (Nelson and Sons, Edinburgh) p. 59.

Cambridge

PRINTED BY C. J. CLAY M.A. AND SONS
AT THE UNIVERSITY PRESS

www.ingramcontent.com/pod-product-compliance
Lightning Source LLC
Chambersburg PA
CBHW021812230426
43669CB00008B/727